THE VISITORS

AMERICAN CHAPTERS

GRETA GORSUCH

西雅图 Seattle
2020·10·2 Britney

WAYZGOOSE PRESS

ISBN: 978-1938757785

Book Design and Editing by Maggie Sokolik, Wayzgoose Press

Cover Design by DJ Rogers, Book Branders

CONTENTS

NOTES ON THE USE OF TWO WORDS IN THIS STORY

The Visitors is set in 1933 in Wellington, Texas. As I wrote this story, I came to a difficult decision. In order to write about *all* the people who lived in Wellington, I would have to use two words, "colored" and "Negro."

"Colored" was a term used by many Americans before the 1850s until the early 1960s. The word "colored" was used to refer to African Americans. In other words, people whose ancestors came from Africa. The term "Negro" was used by many Americans from the 17th century until the early 1970s. Again, the term meant African Americans. In the 1960s and 1970s, many social changes took place in the United States that caused many Americans to rethink these words. Both words fell out of use.

These words are no longer used in polite conversation, and have no place in modern society, nor in modern English use. Both terms are hurtful, and should never be used. To understand more about why these terms are hurtful, please see my historical notes at the end of this story.

ONE

CAITLIN HODGES

I think it all started with that blue ball. I had a lot of arguments with my friend Jilly about this.

Jilly told me, "Our troubles didn't start with a blue ball. The only *one* who's seen it is you."

"Bill Healy saw it," I said. "He saw it way on the south side of town. Mabel Entringer saw it, too. But she saw it outside the colored school. That's on the north side of town, near us."

"Perfect," Jilly said. "An old drunk and some colored woman."

I had no answer to that. I liked Bill. I liked Mabel, too. I had seen the ball a dozen times in just one week. It was just a medium-sized ball. It was bigger than a baseball but a little smaller than a basketball. A child on a beach might play with a blue ball like that. You saw that color, and it meant h-o-l-i-d-a-y. I don't know where I got the idea. I'd never seen a beach. I'd never seen an ocean. Wellington was far away from anything like that. In 1933, we had dust and sand. We had lots of wind, but no beaches, and no ocean. There was no water, really. It hadn't rained since March. Now it was June, and getting hot.

The first time I saw that bouncing blue ball, I was on my way to school. My little brother James was late. He had a spelling test he didn't want to take. He could not spell at all. Mother told me I had to wait for him. I stood at our front gate and stepped out into the dirt road.

"Caitlin!" Mother called. "I told you to wait!" I stepped back inside the gate. I waited. One...two...three...four...five... Then I stepped back out onto the road again. "Caitlin!" Mother called out. I couldn't see her. Where was she? How did she do that? How could she even see me? Back I went inside the gate. One...two... Then back outside the gate. I wanted to get going.

The third or fourth time this happened, I saw the blue ball bounce right past me. Where did it come from? I was so surprised that I didn't hear Mother call. I leaned over to see better. A blue rubber ball, impossible to miss, was bouncing down the road to school. A good strong wind was behind it. It was moving fast. It bounced high, and then zipped along the red dirt road. Could I catch it? I liked that blue color. Like the big blue ball on a Quaker Oats box. I was about to run after it when I felt a hand on my shoulder.

"Caitlin?" Mother said.

"Aaah!" I said, surprised. Mother laughed.

"Uh huh," she said.

"How do you do that?" I said. My mother had the quietest walk of anyone I knew. "Is there anyone you can't sneak up on?"

"No," she said. I believed her.

She handed me a brown bag. It was James' lunch. "James isn't going to school. Why don't you give this to Mabel Entringer if you see her? It's a good lunch. Someone at her school might want it. It's on your way."

"Oh, all right," I said. Mother kissed me on the cheek. She went through the gate and watched me leave for school. I wanted to find that blue ball. It couldn't have gotten far. But there wasn't anything to stop it. Wellington, Texas, was as flat as a pancake. That ball could bounce along forever.

That was the first time I saw the blue ball. I saw it again and again for another week.

It just sat there in the road, or in front of the colored school, or at a gas station. The wind would blow, and it would shiver a little, like it was cold. Then off it bounced. Every time I saw it, I thought about catching it, but I didn't try. It got so I enjoyed seeing it. I never knew where it would show up.

TWO

MARIAN HODGES

I came to think of that week in June, 1933 as a circus. Why a circus? Well, you might think a circus is a spot of excitement. You can look forward to it. There are horses, and clowns, and tents with bright flags. You can walk around the circus in a falling evening light. The light goes blue and pale, and the circus lights come on, beautiful and soft. You can feel that everything is fine, and that you have nothing else to do for the rest of the night. You can see your neighbors, also walking, and enjoying the evening. Even if your week has been dull and you've washed too many dishes and clothes and children, a circus can change all that.

A circus is also a big mess. The circus comes to town on a train. If you have business at the train station that day, you can forget it. It's best to stay away. There are dozens of circus people walking around and shouting. No one knows where anything is. There are animals in cages. There are boxes everywhere. Trucks line up at the station to take the circus out to the north edge of town.

In Wellington, Texas, that means the trucks drive right up

our street. Our street is just plain dirt. After many months without rain, the dirt is deep, and dry. A circus means my little house gets full of dirt. The trucks pass by, raising clouds of red, dry dirt. Closing the windows doesn't help. I tried that. Of course, anyone who owns a truck is happy to get the work. The last circus that came through needed twelve trucks to move their people and their boxes and their animals. Even my husband drove a truck for the circus once. He made four dollars. In 1933, work was scarce, and money was even scarcer.

So, a circus? A spot of excitement, yes. A big mess, oh yes. A circus is what we got when Bonnie Parker and Clyde Barrow came to little Wellington, Texas, on Saturday, June 10, 1933. They came in their big stolen car around sunset after a long, bright day. They bought gas at the D.C.D. #2 gas station right on the highway. They drove out of town fast. They didn't want anyone to see them, I guess. Then, just a few minutes north of town, Clyde drove his car into a river. He was going too fast. He wasn't watching. The big car looked ruined.

You could say Bonnie was ruined, too. I heard she got trapped in the car. She couldn't get out. Somehow, I don't know how, she got some very bad burns on her legs. She was in pain for the rest of her short life. Clyde went to get help. But Clyde, being Clyde, did the kind of thing Clyde Barrow always did. Things went bad. Then the messy, crazy circus really began. I'll let my husband Tom tell that part. He works for the newspaper. He wrote the story of what happened after Clyde Barrow drove that stolen car into the Salt Fork of the Red River.

The strange thing is, that week I really thought a circus *was* coming to town. I was doing laundry. Washing clothes and sheets and towels was tough work. I had to do most of it by hand. With Tom, my husband, Caitlin, my daughter, and James, my son, there was a lot of washing to do. I was hanging some sheets out to dry behind my house. Then, I saw a flash of blue out on the road. That wasn't a color you often saw. The country was dry. There was no rain for months. Everything looked brown, or red, and where there was water, a little green—but not bright blue.

I left my laundry behind and walked over the brown, dead grass to our front gate. There sat a bright blue ball. It was just a medium-sized ball. It sat in the deep red dust of the road. I thought, "Is a circus coming to town?" I don't know where that idea came from. I guess the ball just looked so bright and pretty. It was like looking at an evening out, all the work of the day done. I looked up and down the street. If a circus had come to town, there would be dozens of trucks going down my road. All that dust--I had to bring my sheets out of the back yard. But, there weren't any trucks. It was just an ordinary, hot morning in Wellington. All was quiet.

Then, a strong wind blew out of the north. Before I knew it, the ball bounced high in the air and rolled fast toward town. The last I saw it, it was already past 7th Street and rolling out of sight.

THREE

CAITLIN HODGES

I was already late for school, and looking for Mabel Entringer. Mother told me to give James' lunch to her. Mabel worked at the Negro school just a block north of our house.

Every morning she walked by our house to get there. She had a job making meals for the kids at the school. I heard her tell Mother she was a "nutritionist." That was what she called it. I liked the sound of that word: nutritionist. I wanted to do something like that when I grew up.

I walked to school with my books, my lunch, and James' lunch. Maybe I would pass Mabel on the way. What luck, I saw her just a block away! I called out, "Mrs. Entringer! Mabel! Mabel!" I saw her smile. I ran up to her. My shoes raised clouds of dust from the road.

Mabel coughed and waved her hand in front of her face, from the dust. "You're in a hurry," she said. She wore a blue dress and a large straw hat, which protected her from the sun.

"I'm late for school," I said. "I had to wait for James, but then he didn't come downstairs. He's staying at home. Mother asked me to give you this." I handed her the brown paper lunch bag.

"What's this?" she asked.

"It's James' lunch," I said. "It's a ham sandwich. And..." I looked into my own lunch bag.

"And...an apple," I finished. Then I gave her my apple, too. Apples weren't my favorite.

"Oh," Mabel said. "Thank you. I know someone who will want this."

I was late for school. I needed to go, but I also wanted to complain to somebody. "James has a spelling test he doesn't want to take. That's why he's staying home from school," I said.

"Oh?" Mabel said. "Is that what you think?"

"Oh yeah," I said.

Mabel looked at me. Her big straw hat gave her a little shade from the early morning sun. Under the hat, I could see her dark brown eyes. Mabel Entringer had a soft voice, but her eyes could be sharp. I was getting a sharp look from her. I thought that maybe it was time for me to go to school.

"Well," Mabel said, finally, "James may not be feeling well. Don't be too quick to complain about others. It won't ever make you happy."

"Uh, okay," I said. First my mother, and now Mabel. I just couldn't catch a break today. Do this. Do that. Do the right thing. Say the right thing, not the thing you just said.

Perhaps Mabel saw the unhappy look on my face. She said, "It's all right." I felt a little better. Then she said, "Caitlin Hodges. You're fine. Just think about yourself, now. Enjoy school. Enjoy the day!"

"All right." I said. And then I took off for school. I must

have raised more dust because I heard Mabel coughing and laughing as I ran off.

I passed the Wurtzes' house, and then the Kellerman place. That's where my friend Jilly lived. Right past Jilly's house is where the business section of Wellington started, on 8th Street. Father's newspaper office was there, and so was Powell's Ice Cream Shop and the big Commercial Hotel. It was a Tuesday morning. Downtown should have been a busy place. Farmers used to come into town in their old trucks. Lots of people came in on horseback, too. They'd buy food or tools. People would go in and out of the bank, or get a piece of pie at Reed's Café. But today, downtown Wellington was quiet. I didn't see anyone at all. I couldn't see any trucks or cars.

As I ran past Father's newspaper office, I waved. Maybe he saw me through their big glass windows. I'm not sure.

catch a break = not hitting

FOUR

MABEL ENTRINGER

My name is Mabel Entringer. I was born in Clay County, Missouri. You don't need to know the year. My father was a medical doctor. His name was Michael Johnson. So, I was born Mabel Mae Johnson. I got the name "Entringer" from my husband, Maul, when I married him. After Maul Entringer disappeared, I kept his name. There's been no word for six years, now, but I'm still Mabel Entringer.

My childhood in Missouri was a happy one. I look back at it now and know I was lucky then—very lucky. Our town was friendly. There was money. Both Mother and Father had standing in town. They had important jobs. People looked up to them. I did, too.

Mae was my mother's name. I got my middle name from her. She was the head cook for a hospital in Excelsior Springs, Missouri. She was a small woman, but she walked straight with her shoulders back. She always wore a hat outdoors. She looked taller than she really was.

Dr. Michael Johnson helped colored people and white people alike. Everyone called him "Dr. Mack," which was short for "Michael." We lived right in Excelsior Springs. It was a town with hot springs, and there were plenty of hotels and hospitals. Our hot springs could cure all kinds of sickness. Thousands of people came every year to be cured of something. Sickness hit both whites and coloreds alike. My father said, "Sickness doesn't see the color of your skin." My father was called to the Elms Hotel, the Snapp Hotel, the Excelsior Springs Hospital, and half a dozen other places every week. If he couldn't walk to a place, he went by horseback.

I learned a lot from my father and mother. From my father, I learned people with sore knees and feet and hands and shoulders had "arthritis." Patients who coughed and had fevers might have "a common cold" or "influenza." During one long hot summer, many of his patients were children. He was a happy man, laughing and joking—but not that summer. Many of those children came down with a fever and a terrible headache. They had trouble breathing and moving their legs. Father called it "polio."

Dr. Mack had some success with those children. He had them lie down in the hot springs. Then, he taught their mothers and fathers to stretch and rub their children's legs. He gave the children breathing lessons.

"Breathe in... in... in... four, five, six, seven, AND OUT... out... out... four, five, six, seven," he said, in his deep voice. The children would never be completely cured, but they might still be able to use their legs and walk again.

From my mother I learned about how to make healthy food. She taught me how to preserve vegetables, so we could eat them even in the winter. We grew tomatoes all summer, and then we washed them well. We cut them up and put them in clean glass jars. Then, we put the open jars in boiling water for an hour. We let everything cool off, and then we sealed the jars very, very carefully. During the winter, we could open a jar and breathe in that beautiful summer smell of fresh tomatoes. They were so good to eat!

That was twenty years ago. Now, I'm a grown woman. I live in Wellington, Texas, far from my old hometown in Missouri. I use the things my mother taught me every day, both at home and at work. Today, at the Booker T. Washington School, I planned to teach the older girls how to preserve vegetables. I carried a bag of tomatoes for the girls to use.

FIVE

MABEL ENTRINGER

On my way to school, I ran into little Caitlin Hodges. She is such a smart child, and quick to talk and move. Her mother, Marian Hodges, was my first friend in Wellington.

Caitlin was walking and talking faster than she should. She was always like that. When I saw her on the road, she was like a talking cloud of dust. I made a big show of waving my hand in front of my face. I enjoyed Caitlin. She was like a ball of energy. Today, that wasn't such a good thing, with all the red dust. It hadn't rained in days. I gently pulled her out of the road and out of the dust. A young girl from a good family shouldn't be standing in the middle of the road to talk. Mother taught me that. There was a little shade under a tree nearby. We stood under the tree while I listened to Caitlin. She talked about her mother, and her brother James. She said something about James staying home from school.

Somewhere in the middle her talk, Caitlin gave me a present of a ham sandwich and two fresh green apples. Did I know someone at school who wanted them? I told her I certainly did. Marian Hodges' ham sandwiches were good. Cal

Meade, our handyman at the school, was not eating well. The home-cooked lunch would do him good. We had a few people at school who were not eating well. They never said so, but I could tell. They didn't have any energy, and they were thin.

Times were hard. There wasn't much work. Some of our students and staff went hungry a few days a week. No one's garden was doing that well with no rain. I watered my tomatoes and mustard plants by hand. I had a good, deep, water well at my house. I pumped the water, and filled up my buckets. Then I carried the buckets of water to each plant. One cup of water at a time, I kept my plants alive. Even so, the tomatoes I carried this morning were small and hard, and smelled sharp. They didn't get enough water.

It was my job to cook for the students and teachers at Booker T. Washington School. An even bigger part of my job was finding food to cook with. Marian Hodges and her husband, Tom, helped. Marian went to her friends in town and asked them for food donations. Some gave cans of food. I once got a big bag of flour from some women from the church. Old Mr. Sykes killed a hog last year. He gave us a whole ham from that hog. Tom Hodges put up a sign asking for food donations in the front window of the newspaper office where he worked. People, both white and Negro, would stop by with bread and vegetables and butter for "the colored school." That's what people in town called the Booker T. Washington School.

Finally, Caitlin ran out of talk. We said goodbye and she ran off toward the white school. She left a cloud of red dust behind her. I started walking toward my school, in the opposite direction. I passed by the Hodges' house. I didn't see Marian, and anyway, I couldn't stop. My bags were heavy, and the sun was bright and hot, even at eight in the morning.

As I got close to school, I slowed down. There was a small group of trees that I liked to stand under. I don't know why, but that little place was like green heaven. Maybe there was just a little water there. Water you couldn't see. The trees gave shade, and the grass grew long and green and soft underneath.

This morning I saw something strange. A medium-sized blue ball sat in the deep grass. It was the color that caught my eye. I don't know where it came from. I didn't know any children in town who had a ball like that.

The ball was covered in red dust from the road. I picked it up and looked it over. There was no name on it. It was so pretty and blue. It was soft. I brushed the red dust off, and then I put the blue ball back down into the tall green grass. It was time for work. I had to go.

SIX

TOM HODGES

Every morning that week of June 1933 started out the same way—slowly. No one came to the newspaper office. That meant the newspaper wasn't selling advertising. We needed the money from advertising. Even the big D.C.D. gas station chain wasn't buying advertising. The only ads we ran last week were for Fatimah cigarettes, the Cox Meat Market, and the Wellington State Bank. The bank wanted our readers to open up new savings accounts. At the time, no one had money to save. They had no reason to trust a bank.

The slow mornings meant I was free to clean up the mess from the night before. I put away loose pieces of type. I wiped up black ink from the floor. I wiped and cleaned the big newspaper press in back. That was the best part of my job. I knew newspaper presses. I knew how to make them run. I loved their big machine smell. It was like metal and oil and wood and electricity, all together.

Around three each afternoon, we were busy putting the next day's newspaper together. Mr. Roger Elms, the owner, came in his big green truck. We shut the front office, and Mr.

Elms and I put together our stories and news for the day. We put national and international news first, then state news, and finally local news. We had to figure out where to put all three of our advertisements for the week. It wasn't hard to do. The ads were small, and could go anywhere. Then we started setting type. We picked up pieces of type, sometimes letters, sometimes whole words like *the*, and put them in place. That took two or three hours.

Then Bill Healy came by around five. He knocked on the front door and we let him in. He was the night help. Bill had what my wife Marian called "a drinking problem." Three hours a day at the newspaper office was the only work he could find. I thought he was all right. He was always clear-eyed at work. He never smelled of alcohol. You wouldn't think he was a drinking man. Lucky for us, he was all right with heavy lifting. He didn't mind getting black newspaper ink on his hands and clothes. He'd worked for a newspaper in Dallas, he said. I don't know how he ended up in a small town like Wellington.

Once we got the type set for all eight pages of the newspaper, Bill set up the rolls of paper next to the newspaper press. I got the press running, and then things got really noisy as well as busy. There is nothing noisier than a newspaper press. I loved it. In another hour, we finished our press run of 1,300 copies. Mr. Elms came out of his office to help us stack the newspapers and tie them into bundles.

Cal Meade, the handyman at the Negro school near my house came by around 6:30 in the evening. He worked a few extra hours for the newspaper at night. Together, Cal and Bill piled the newspaper bundles into the back of Mr. Elms' truck. Then they drove the truck to three delivery places in town. One was in the north part of town. That was the poor area.

There were a few nice houses, but rich people didn't live there. The second delivery spot was in the south part of town. That area had more businesses and big houses. If you were rich like the Wurtzes, the Kellermans, or the Rowes, that's where you lived. The third delivery spot was out on the big north-south highway, Highway 83. That was on the east side of town. Highway 83 was the way in and out of Wellington.

Around seven o'clock, my daughter Caitlin came to bring me home for dinner. She didn't have to, but it was just something we liked to do together. It was only a ten-minute walk. That Thursday night, Mr. Elms told me he had to leave town for a few days. He said something about his mother in Dallas, and how he had to see her. He'd be back Monday morning, he said. I told him everything would be fine. I'd open the newspaper office Friday and Saturday morning as usual.

Little Caitlin and I walked home after that. It was still hot, but the shadows were getting long. The sun was setting. The whole world looked red.

SEVEN

BILL HEALY

Cal and I got all the newspapers into the back of Mr. Elms' truck. We're both strong, so it didn't take long. I tossed them to Cal and Cal tossed them into the truck. There weren't many newspaper bundles to load. Mr. Elms had money trouble, just like everyone else. I heard him tell Tom Hodges that ten years ago in 1923, he sold 3,500 newspapers a day.

The county was full of people then. Everyone wanted cheap land. They wanted to try their luck at farming. For a few years, it worked. People came in from Oklahoma, Iowa, Kansas, and Louisiana. There was rain, and people grew cotton, corn, and millet. They kept hogs and cattle. Then the banks crashed in 1929. That was the start of our troubles. Everyone lost their savings, and then things got worse. Businesses failed.

Now, a lot of people think the rain stopped falling in 1929, too. It was like they thought 1929 was a complete disaster. The year 1929 *was* a disaster. Men like me lost everything. Everyone lost out. But, the part about the rain is not true. After I came out to Wellington, I kept track of the rain. I don't know why. I'm not a farmer—I just like to measure things. I pay attention to things around me. I set up a little tin cup outside. I painted the cup white. I drew numbers on the side of the cup with a little blue paint and a fine brush. One eighths of an inch, two eighths of an inch, and so on. When the cup caught rain, I could measure how much fell.

In 1930, Wellington had 20 inches of rain. In 1931, there was 19 inches. In 1932, we had a great year—28 inches of rain! The rain was fine, but cotton prices were so low that no one could make any money. Everyone was hoping 1933 would turn everything around. 1933 would be an end to our troubles —good rain and good prices for farmers. But to be honest, 1933 wasn't looking so good. We were not getting rain, and that's a fact. By June, there were only four inches of rain. April and May were supposed to be rainy months, but not this year.

Thursday night, Tom Hodges' little girl Caitlin came to get her dad for dinner, as usual. We always talked a little while she waited. I mostly listened. Sometimes she talked about school, or about how their radio was broken and they couldn't get it fixed. Tonight, she was quiet. She helped Cal and me count the bundles of newspapers. Thump! Thump! Thump! One by one they went into the truck.

"I count thirteen hundred, Mr. Healy," Caitlin said.

"That's what I got too," I said. "Whew!" Cal and I stopped to rest. It was still hot. Then little Caitlin said something I couldn't hear. "What's that, honey?" I said.

"Watch out for that blue ball," she said.

Now, I understood the words she said. "Watch out for that blue ball," she said. I couldn't put any of it together. Blue ball? What blue ball?

"I don't get what you mean, honey," I said.

So then she says she's seen a blue ball bouncing around

the streets of Wellington. She saw it in front of her house, bouncing along with the wind behind it. She saw it again down by Powell's Ice Cream Shop. She saw it by the movie theater a day later. Then she saw it near her school.

"I thought some kid would grab it at school, for sure. It's so pretty! But no one seemed to see it. It was behind a tree, I guess. It was just outside the school yard. I walked over to it but the wind picked it up again. It just bounced away," she said.

"What's it like? A basketball?" I asked her.

"No, it's a little smaller," she said. "Like a beach ball."

"A beach ball," I said.

"Yes," she said. I didn't have an answer to that.

Finally, I said, "Well, I'll look out for it, then." Caitlin just nodded. Then her father came to get her. The last I saw them, they were walking home.

Cal started the truck. I climbed in beside him. We took newspapers to three spots—one north, one south, and one down on the big highway. I wasn't thinking of anything special. It was just a hot, late afternoon. But then as we drove to our last stop, I saw it. It was the strangest thing. I had to laugh. Next to the highway was a blue ball. It sat like a big blue egg in the brown grass. It was clear as day.

Cal looked at me, but I just shook my head. "Never mind," I said. "Just something I saw."

EIGHT

CAITLIN HODGES

Father and I walked home. He wasn't moving too fast, so I just slowed down and we walked together. I have to say, we didn't raise as much red dust that way. I don't think he was tired or anything. He was just enjoying the sunset. It cooled off, little by little. The shadows got longer. The hard, bright, high blue sky got softer, and somehow closer in. You could reach it.

Mother left a special broom on our front porch. Anytime Father, James, and I came home, we used it to brush the road dust off our shoes and legs. When we got home I brushed off first. Then Father brushed off, and we went in our front door. The big screen door gave a bang as it closed behind us.

Mother called from the kitchen, "Dinner's on the table!"

Father walked back to the kitchen. I could hear Mother and Father talking. Mother laughed at something Father said.

Then Father called to me, "Caitlin! Tell James dinner is ready."

"Okay!" I said.

I went to the bottom of the stairs to call up to James, but

then I thought better of it. I went up the stairs, two at a time. Going somewhere or doing something was easier for me than yelling.

James had stayed home for three days now. I wanted to see what was wrong with him. Staying home one day because of a spelling test was one thing. Staying home three days from school was another.

When I got to James' room, he was in bed. His window was open. He wasn't moving. He didn't say anything. That was strange. James didn't like me to be in his room. By now, he should have said, "Caitlin!" or "What are you doing in here? Get out!" Typical little brother stuff.

"James?" I said. He didn't answer. I went into his room. "James?" I said, louder. I touched his shoulder. He was burning hot. I could feel it through his pajamas. Then it was like he woke up a little. His eyes opened a little and he said, "Water."

"Right," I said. "I'll get Mother." James nodded. I was down the stairs in two seconds. I got to the dining room where Father was sitting, waiting for dinner. He was looking over the newspaper he'd brought home.

"Father!" I said. "James is so hot! He wants water." I went into the kitchen for a glass of water to take up. Mother went past me, out of the kitchen. She and Father got up the stairs, one after the other. Carrying the glass of water, I climbed the stairs after them. I went a little more slowly this time. I didn't want to spill the water. I was also a little scared. What was wrong with James? When I got to James' room, Father stood in front of the door. He wouldn't let me in. He took the glass of water.

"Caitlin," he said. "Go downstairs. Your mother wants you to turn off the stove. Wait down there a little, all right?" Then he shut James' door. I looked at the closed door for a few minutes. What was going on?

I went downstairs. I went into the kitchen and turned off the stove. A pot of potatoes and green beans was boiling. I got the potatoes out of the pot and put them a bowl. I did the same thing with the green beans. I liked green beans. Mother wasn't there to see, so I ate one. I hardly tasted it.

I heard voices upstairs. James' door opened. Father came downstairs and left through the front door. After another minute, he started up his truck. That was not a good sign. He didn't use the truck unless he had to. Gas cost too much money. This meant only one thing: he was going to get the doctor. James was really sick.

Mother called down the stairs. "Caitlin!" she said.

"Can I come upstairs?" I asked.

"Not now honey," Mother said. "Not until we know what's wrong with James."

"Oh," I said. I had not thought of that.

Then Mother said, "Just take the potatoes and beans out of the pot and put them into a bowl."

"I already did that," I said.

"That's my girl," Mother said. "There's some chicken already on the table. Why don't you have something to eat? Just one piece of chicken, though." Then I heard James' door close.

"All right," I said to no one. I didn't feel like eating. I went outside. It was almost dark now. I waited until the stars came out, one by one. I waited some more, until Father came home in his truck. The doctor came a few minutes later in his car.

NINE

TOM HODGES

The doctor went upstairs to see my boy. I went to the back-yard pump to wash my hands.

I called to little Caitlin, "Caitlin! Bring some soap back here. Let's wash up!"

She came out with a little piece of soap and a white towel. Caitlin pumped the water while I washed up. Then, I pumped the water for her. I made her wash her hands twice. She made a face, but she did it anyway. I didn't know what was wrong with her little brother. James was burning with fever. I never saw him so sick. I didn't want Caitlin to get sick, too.

Caitlin and I sat at our dining room table and ate a little. We weren't very hungry. We could hear voices upstairs in James' room. Caitlin looked a little scared, so I picked up tomorrow's newspaper that I brought home. We liked to read it together, to check for mistakes, or to talk about anything interesting in the news.

I read some news aloud for Caitlin. One of the stories was about the gangsters Clyde Barrow and Bonnie Parker. No one knew where they were. Yet everyone wanted to talk about them. The police wanted them for killings, stealing cars, and robbing banks.

The idea of a young man and woman breaking the law together was exciting to some people. A newspaper in Missouri got some photos that Bonnie and Clyde had taken. A week later, we printed two of the photos in our little Wellington newspaper. They showed Bonnie in a little dress with a hat. She was smoking a cigar and holding a shotgun. Some people thought she looked modern or special. In his picture, Clyde wore an expensive suit and hat. He carried a pistol. You couldn't see his eyes.

Bonnie Parker and Clyde Barrow didn't seem exciting to me. They were just a couple of unlucky kids from Dallas. They could be any of us. Except most of us tried to do our best. We didn't steal money or cars. We worked at hard jobs for long hours. Still, I lived and breathed newspapers. Bonnie and Clyde were news.

In another way, there was something dark about those two. They didn't just steal cars and money. Clyde Barrow was too fast with a gun. People ended up dead. I didn't think that a pair of gangsters like them were glamorous or exciting. They were dangerous.

According to the newspaper I read to Caitlin, Clyde killed two policemen in Missouri last April. Bonnie, Clyde, and some other men were hiding out in a small house. They were loud, and played cards late into the night. People who lived nearby called the police. When the police came to see what was happening, Clyde started shooting. Two policemen were killed. Bonnie and Clyde sped off in a stolen car.

I know some people thought little girls like Caitlin shouldn't hear about killing. I didn't hide things from Caitlin.

She was too smart. I was just a newspaperman—I tell the truth for a living.

Caitlin asked me, "Where are Bonnie and Clyde now?"

"No one knows, honey," I said. "It says that the police are looking for them in Oklahoma, Texas, and Missouri."

"Could they come here?" Caitlin asked.

That question made me sit up. Clyde Barrow knew Wellington. Before he turned really bad, he worked here picking cotton. Lots of hard-luck families from Dallas came out here in July and August to pick cotton. It was really terrible work. It ruined your hands, but it paid well. The pickers lived in wagons and tents. When the cotton was picked, they all went back to Dallas, or Longview, or wherever.

Old Raney Lord, a cotton farmer north of here, told me Clyde worked for him once. He told me, "Clyde was only fifteen then, but he already had a mouth on him. He sat around after lunch, taking his time. I told him to get back to work, and he told me 'No broke-down cotton farmer is going to tell me what to do.' I paid him for the day, and then told him to get off my land. He did—but not before he stole a pair of boots."

Caitlin's question was a good one. Clyde knew this country. There weren't that many people living out here now. There were lots of empty houses outside of town. Hundreds of farmers had run out of money, given up, and moved away. The country around here was a perfect place for Clyde Barrow and Bonnie Parker to hide. They could show up for a visit.

Caitlin said, "Father?"

"Nothing, Caitlin. Bonnie and Clyde won't show up here," I said. At that moment, the doctor and Marian came downstairs.

TEN

MARIAN HODGES

Thursday night seemed very long. The doctor came and went. My boy James still had a high fever. The doctor told me it was probably nothing—maybe a bad summer cold. The fever was a natural thing, the doctor said.

"The fever helps burn out the sickness," he said, as he closed his black doctor's bag. "If the fever doesn't go down in a few hours, give him some of this in water." He handed me a small packet of white powder. "It's aspirin."

My husband Tom brought me a big glass of water and a plate of food. "James can't eat any of that," I said. Tom put the plate in my hand and said, "It's for you, honey."

It was now Friday morning. I heard my husband, Tom, get Caitlin some breakfast. He got her dressed and out the door to school. She stopped at James' bedroom door before she left.

"Mother?" she called. She kept her voice soft.

"Don't open the door, Caitlin," I called back, just as softly. "The doctor doesn't know what's wrong with James yet. I don't want you getting sick, too."

"Okay," Caitlin said. Then she left for school. When I went

out a few minutes later, I found a green apple just outside the door. For a second, I felt like crying. My little Caitlin was a smart girl, and always ready to give. I picked up the apple and took a bite. I was hungry. I'd stayed up all night with James. Around five, his fever broke, without the aspirin. He was sleeping deeply now, two hours later.

I thought the doctor didn't really know what was wrong with James. He said something that made me feel cold inside. He said, "If he has trouble moving his legs or neck, come get me right away." Did he think James had polio? Polio killed people. When it didn't kill, someone who had polio would never be the same again. Our president, Franklin Roosevelt, got polio. He never walked again. He was lucky to be alive.

I needed to go downstairs and clean up, and think about making lunch. Would James be hungry now, with his fever gone? I might make some chicken soup. As I left James' room, he woke up. He said a few things I couldn't understand. It sounded like fever talk. Then he said, clear as a bell: "Mother, where's the circus?"

I went back to his bed. "What, James?" I asked.

He said, sleepily, "There's a circus coming—with animals and candy."

I didn't know what to say. I hadn't heard a circus was coming. That would be big news in Wellington. Tom hadn't told me anything. Working at the newspaper, he would know. With no rain, and no jobs, people in Wellington could use a night at the circus. It was something fun to do in the evening, and maybe there would be some work to get the circus moved from the train station out to the open fields north of town. We could use the money. I started to tell James I would find out, but he had already fallen back asleep.

I went downstairs to clean up the kitchen. Then I changed

my clothes and washed my face. I combed my hair and put it up with hairpins. I saw myself in the mirror by the front door. I looked like any other woman—a mother, a wife, hair pulled up, white apron over a blue dress. I looked like a woman whose hands were always damp from washing dishes or clothes.

How had I gotten here? Just twelve years before, I was a big town girl in Oklahoma City. I worked for my father's paper company. Then I met Tom Hodges. He was a newspaper printer. He wanted to be a reporter. He visited Father's paper company to find a better paper for his newspaper press.

I liked Tom right away. He was not too tall, with dark hair and gray eyes. He had nice voice that was not loud. We got married in Oklahoma City, and then we had Caitlin and James. Five years ago, Tom got a job at a small newspaper in Wellington, Texas. He thought it was a job he could grow into. He hoped to become a reporter. It was close to Oklahoma. I could visit, if I wanted to.

At first, everything seemed fine. Wellington was okay. It was small compared to Oklahoma City. That bothered me. There weren't too many places to go. But, I made friends. I met Mabel Entringer, who was also new to town. My little girl Caitlin loved Wellington. It seems like she knew every corner of it. She had friends of every age. She could talk to just about everyone.

Then, like a black storm on a blue sunny day, the banks failed. My mother and father lost all their money back in Oklahoma City. Father lost his business. He died. Mother went to Kansas City to live with my brother. Tom's pay was cut by one quarter. The newspaper wasn't doing well. We got used to eating meat only two or three times a week. Then it stopped raining.

Sometimes I wondered why I was here in this little lonely town where no one had money. I felt like a visitor in this wide open country without trees or water or anything green. It was like I was sitting in a big empty train station. I was waiting to leave, but the train never came.

I couldn't go on thinking like this. My son's fever was gone. I had a husband and two beautiful children. I went outside to get some fresh air. It wasn't too hot yet. The sun was low in the eastern sky.

I walked to the back of my house where I had planted a few small trees. They probably needed water. I got a bucket and went to our water pump. There, right by our pump, sat a bright blue ball. It had to be the one I'd seen the other day. How did it get here? The last I saw it, it was bouncing off toward town with a strong wind behind it.

ELEVEN

MARIAN HODGES

I bent over to pick the ball up. It was the same ball, I'm sure of it. It was soft and bright blue. There wasn't even any red dust on it. It wasn't heavy. I thought of a circus again. That was just James' fever talk, I'm sure.

A circus would be nice. Looking at the ball made me think about that. I took it to our back door. I would give it to James when he woke up. I went back to watering my little trees.

The wind picked up again out of the south. I felt a wave of heat as the sun rose higher in the sky. I gave each tree two buckets of water. I poured them slowly. The water went deep into the soil, down to the roots. I heard someone call my name from the street.

"Marian! Marian!"

My shoes crunched on the dead dry grass as I came around the house to our front gate. Mabel Entringer waved from the gate. I was glad to see her. She was on her way to work at the colored school. It was just a few streets north of us.

I asked her to come inside the gate so we could talk. She wore a hat and a nice dress. She had an extra bag on her arm. She gave me the bag. "It's just some chicken soup," she said, in her soft, educated voice. "I had a little extra. I thought you could use it."

"How did you know?" I said. I looked inside the bag. There was a glass jar full of golden chicken soup. I couldn't believe it. Chicken soup was exactly what James needed.

"Oh, I saw Caitlin yesterday. She said James wasn't feeling well. She called it his 'spelling test sickness.'" We both laughed. Caitlin had a way of talking that was sharp and funny.

Mabel continued, "I thought James might be truly sick. So I brought the soup." She looked at me. "You look tired. Were you up late last night?"

"Yes, I was. But James' fever broke a few hours ago. He's asleep now," I said.

"Maybe you should have some of the soup, too," Mabel said. I laughed. I did feel hungry.

I said, "The doctor doesn't know what's wrong with James. He said to call if James had trouble moving his legs."

Mabel looked shocked. Her kind brown eyes were wide. We stopped talking for just a minute. "Not polio?" she said quietly.

"The doctor didn't say so, but he must be thinking about it," I said.

"After James wakes up, have him push his foot against your hand—one leg at a time. If he can push hard against your hand, and if both legs can push hard, he probably doesn't have polio," Mabel said.

"Oh!" I said. "I didn't know that."

"It's a trick my father, Doctor Mack, uses back in Missouri," Mabel said.

"I'd like to meet him some day," I said. "You must miss him."

"I do," said Mabel. "But with money so tight, the way things are…" She stopped talking.

I knew she was saying she didn't have the money to visit Excelsior Springs. No one had the money to do things like that, really.

I never knew how Mabel came to Wellington, or, why she stayed. I knew we both arrived here at the same time. She'd been married to a man, a truck driver. Was his name Paul, or Maul, or something? I think he was from Wellington. I'm not sure. All I knew was he never returned six years ago. No one ever heard from him again. No one ever saw the truck again. Mabel visited the sheriff in Wellington, and told him her husband was late by two days. She went again, many times. Sometimes I went with her, but it made no difference. They never found anything.

Sheriff Black called the sheriff in Dallas, where Mabel's husband was supposed to go with a truck full of cotton, potatoes, and onions. The sheriff in Dallas didn't even spend five minutes talking to Sheriff Black. He said he couldn't keep track of every Negro truck driver who was driving around the state of Texas. He said he was probably just trucking whiskey around, anyway. Or, he ran into trouble. Someone might have taken his truck, taken the whiskey. He said he might have gotten tired of his wife and ran off somewhere else with his truck.

Sheriff Black never said that last part to Mabel. I heard it from my husband Tom, who went to Sheriff Black later. He wanted to write a story on Mabel's missing husband. Tom wrote a short story for the Wellington newspaper. Mr. Elms agreed to print it. Tom sent the story to the Dallas newspapers, too, but not one newspaper there printed the story.

Mabel's husband would never drive whiskey around. I believed her when she said that. I also didn't believe he left her. Mabel was beautiful and smart. She came from a good family. Something bad happened to Mabel's husband on that trip to Dallas. We might never find out what happened.

Mabel and I talked a few minutes more. She needed to go to work. I wanted to check on James. I went around to the back of the house to get the blue ball to take up to him. Maybe he would be awake.

The ball was gone. Did the wind pick up it again and take it somewhere? I spent a few minutes looking around, but I never saw it again.

TWELVE

CAITLIN HODGES

I spent school lunch arguing with Jilly Kellerman about the best books we had ever read. Jilly liked *Emil and the Detectives*.

"That story about the little kid in Germany?" I said.

"Yeah," said Jilly. "I love the pictures. I want to visit Berlin! Someday I will. Emil has friends, and together they find a spy at a hotel, and they catch him."

Then she said, like she always did, at least twice a day, "My grandma and grandpa came from Germany." She always lifted her head a little when she said that. It was true. Her grandma and grandpa did come from Germany. They started a bank in Wellington. Jilly's father, their only son, was the bank president. Jilly and her family lived in the biggest house in town.

"What about a book with more adventure?" I asked. "Something out of this world? Something strange!"

"Like what?" Jilly asked.

"*The Midnight Folk*," I said. "It's about a boy, Kay Harker. He lives by himself at a big country house. His great-grandpa was a sea captain and..."

Jilly's eyes grew round. She loved any story about the

ocean. Neither of us had seen the ocean, of course. We'd heard about it. It was big and blue. There was a lot of water, with birds and fish and a sand beach to run and play on. The idea of it was so exciting.

"Girls!" called the teacher. "Come in! Lunch is over!"

"Aww," I said. "Just when it was getting interesting." We went into the big red brick school building. Over the door were the words, "Wellington Elementary School."

Wellington spent a lot of money on that school, I heard Father tell Mother once. It was true that Wellington mostly had dirt roads. But, the road in front of the school was paved with brick. This meant less red dust. We had a big library where Jilly and I found all the books we could ever read.

My school was not the same school Mabel Entringer worked at. Negro children went to the Booker T. Washington School. The Negro families in town built the Booker T. Washington School by themselves. It had only two rooms. It was on a dirt road, close to my house. The school did not have a library.

Father and I went there one day. We built some bookshelves. We had some boards, and Father nailed them together to make the shelves. Negro and white families from all over Wellington, and even from Pampa and Dallas, donated books to the colored school. The shelves filled up. But, I could never find a single brand new book among the donations. All the books were used. Someone had written in them, or drew pictures in them, or folded the pages.

Kids at Booker T. Washington school never got to open a book for the first time and smell that wonderful fresh paper and ink smell. It was the same smell Father said he loved when he worked on a big newspaper press. I did, too. Thinking of that, I thought I would go straight to the newspaper office after school. Anyway, James was sick at home, and Mother was busy with him.

I spent the rest of the afternoon sitting with Jilly on one side and Teddy Rangle on the other. Teddy's father had a ranch north of town, on the Salt Fork of the Red River. Teacher made us do math problems, which Teddy and I liked, but Jilly didn't. Then we had to do grammar and spelling, which Jilly liked, but Teddy and I did not.

"How can you love reading books if you can't do grammar and spelling?" Jilly asked.

"I *don't* like reading books," Teddy said. "Just give me a baseball and I'm happy." Jilly slapped Teddy's shoulder. Teddy and I laughed.

"Children," the teacher said. "Silence! Just because it's Friday and there's no school tomorrow, you don't need to act up!"

I whispered to Jilly, "I just like to read. I don't need to pick the words apart!" Jilly just shook her head. Now we had one more thing to argue about.

THIRTEEN

CAITLIN HODGES

When school was over, I asked Jilly and Teddy if they wanted to visit the newspaper office with me. It was hot, even under the trees in front of school. I remembered something from a book about a sunset that read: "That changeful rose color, and purple, and gold of the sunset." The word *changeful* was odd, but I got the feeling of it. The sun in Wellington was still high, and white and bright. No "changeful" sunsets here. Sunset felt hours away. 离落日还有几千小时

Jilly said no. Her mother wanted her at home. She was helping her mother make some new curtains for her room. She said good-bye and walked home with her big sister Bettina. It was funny to watch them cross the road, and then cross back again. They were trying to stay in the shade of trees as they walked. There weren't that many trees in Wellington, so finding shade was hard to do. We watched the two girls, in their new, pretty, perfectly ironed dresses walk away. Jilly's golden curls bounced on her back.

Teddy Rangle said, "Pa doesn't come to town until late, anyway. He wants me to meet him at the bank." It was only four o'clock, so we ran to the newspaper office. I liked Teddy's father. When he had business in town, he came all the way into Wellington from their ranch seven miles to the north. Then he picked Teddy up from school. He rode on *horseback*. A lot of people did that—or they had horses and wagons. But Teddy's father had a beautiful horse, Jacko. He was tall and black. To get on him, Teddy had to climb a fence and then jump on. Once, Teddy's father just reached over from Jacko and pulled Teddy straight up by the back of his coat. One minute Teddy was standing in the road. The next, he was sitting on the back of Jacko behind his pa. Then the two of them rode off home together.

Father was a little surprised to see us at the newspaper office. But he didn't seem unhappy about it. Mr. Elms was gone to Dallas. This meant Father was doing everything by himself. He was behind. When we came in, he was working out the stories to put in the newspaper. Bill Healy was a little late. He was bringing Mr. Elms' truck and it wouldn't start. He was trying to fix it. We had to help Father get the big rolls of paper over to the newspaper press. We helped him prepare the ink. After a pretty busy thirty minutes, Father got the newspaper press started. Over the noise, he shouted, "Just keep an eye on the time! You don't want Teddy late to meet his pa!"

"All right!" I said.

"Stay out of the way while I do this press run!" he shouted. "Why don't you clean up some of this ink from the table here? I didn't have time earlier."

I ran to do it. I was so happy. I loved working in the newspaper office. Teddy came over to help. Together we got the ink off the table. We used two or three newspapers from last week and an old spoon to scrape and wipe. No matter how careful I was, I still got black ink on my old brown and pink dress.

scratch 抓
scrape 刮 剥. 残痕

Teddy laughed at me. I didn't mind. I might get a new dress out of this finally.

Over the roar of the newspaper press, Teddy told me his brother, sister-in-law, and baby niece were visiting for dinner on Saturday. "They're driving in from Pampa!" he shouted. "I get to meet my new baby niece for the first time! Ma and my sisters are all excited." I guess I could see why everyone was excited. But a baby? No thanks. I wasn't interested in babies.

Just then Bill Healy and Cal Meade came in. Bill said, "You already cleaned up good! Did you leave anything for us to do?"

Father called Bill over. The freshly printed newspapers were starting to come off the press. He needed Bill and Cal to begin stacking them. It was five o'clock and Teddy had to go. Over the roar of the newspaper press, he yelled goodbye and ran out the door to meet his father.

I could see Mr. Rangle waiting with Jacko across the street, outside the bank. I looked out the window to get a good look at Jacko. I just loved him. Teddy was so lucky. Then something funny happened. I saw the blue ball. Of course! That ball could show up anywhere. Why not here, and right now?

The sun was starting to go down. There were long shadows from our tall downtown buildings and our few little trees. I saw the bright blue color of the ball as clear as anything. The ball was in Teddy's way when he crossed the street to meet his pa. There was hardly any wind. The ball sat still as if it were waiting. Teddy saw the ball. Who could miss that beach holiday blue ball? Just like he was on the playground at school, he leaned over and picked the ball up. There was no escape for that ball. Not this time. The last time I saw the ball, it was on the back of Jacko, in Teddy's arms, on the way to the Rangle ranch north of town.

FOURTEEN

BILL HEALY

Cal Meade drove the truck up to the back of the newspaper building. "Careful now!" I called out. Cal tended to drive the truck fast. I didn't want him to back into the building and smash the bricks or something. We'd lose our jobs for sure.

It was hot. It felt like that sun would never go down. Oh, it was red and low in the sky, sure. It was strong, though. There was no wind at all. Together, we loaded up the bundles of newspapers. The bundles were heavy. Friday nights, the newspaper had a few more pages. There was more news. Folks wanted to read about things to do on the weekend, like town hall dances and church meetings—anything fun, that didn't cost money, or that took their minds off of the mess this country was in. There were no jobs, no money, and not enough hope. No one wanted to think about having to use their cars less, or losing their farms to the bank.

Cal and I drove off. The truck threw out blue smoke. I hoped it would keep running for at least one more night. I looked back and saw Bill Hodges and little Caitlin close up the newspaper office doors. I supposed they would go home.

We drove to our usual delivery drops. First to the south part of town, and then to the north. The truck stopped once, right in the middle of the street. It took me twenty minutes to get the thing started again. Wellington was completely quiet. I didn't see anyone outside. Cal didn't have much to say. He wasn't a big talker.

We finally made our last drop on Highway 83. Cal pulled up to the D.C.D. #2 gas station and cut off the engine. We got to the back of truck and pulled out our last bundles of newspapers. The manager, Rick Snell, had some boxes set up for us to put the newspapers on.

"Hey Bill!" he called out. I raised my hand to say hi. Six or seven people were already waiting to buy newspapers. The sun slipped down in the west and was gone. It was half dark by now. The few lights of the D.C.D. #2 gas station came on. They made a small pool of yellow light along the dark highway.

It took us a few minutes to get the newspaper bundles out. While we were working, I saw a star come out. Then another. Cal and I rested for a few minutes. I moved the truck over to the pump closest to front door of the gas station. Then I put some gas into the truck. Mr. Elms told me to put in fifty cents' worth. A big fancy car came into the gas station, on the other side of the pump, closest to the highway. I jumped a little. I hadn't seen the car come up. The headlights were not on. I looked a little closer. It was a new car, a big Ford V8. By the looks of it, it was dark red. You didn't see cars like that every day.

The driver got out, a skinny young guy with dark work pants, a rough brown shirt, and big shoes. He wore a cap, just like a kid. He couldn't be more than 16 or 17. I didn't know him. He went into the gas station. The screen door slammed shut.

Through the open windows of the car, I thought I saw a woman sitting in back. She was smoking a cigarette. I saw her hand, in a white glove, flick the ash off her cigarette, out the window closest to me. Then a thin stream of smoke came out of the window into the night air. It's dangerous to smoke near a gas pump. But somehow I just didn't think of that at the time. That big fancy car really had my attention.

I didn't see the second man get out of the car. He must have been really quiet and quick. The man walked around to the back of our truck. I walked back, too, to where Cal Meade was standing. The man went to our last bundle of newspapers. He didn't look up at us. He didn't say a word. He took a knife out of his pocket and cut the string of one bundle, and took a newspaper off the top. Then he just turned around and walked back to his car. He didn't pay Rick Snell the two cents he owed. Yeah, I know it was only two cents, but two cents was two cents. These days, that was a lot.

I called out, "Hey mister!" I felt Cal's hand squeeze my arm, hard. He'd never done that before. "What?" I said. I looked at Cal who looked back at me. He shook his head, a movement so small I hardly saw it. The man was at his car now, ready to get in. He looked straight at us. Now I saw what Cal saw. The man wasn't tall or anything. He was in his twenties. He was slender, and sharply dressed. His dark hair was slicked back. Nothing about him seemed strange, until you looked at his eyes. They were dark, and fixed on us. It made me think of a snake, measuring us, wondering if he could escape, or if he should bite. He had the hardest face I ever saw. Cal's hand squeezed my arm again, and he pulled me back a little, away from the gas pumps, out of the yellow glow of the station lights.

Then the young kid driver came out of the gas station. He was carrying bottles of soda. The older man called out, "C'mon let's go. We'll gas up later." He looked at us again. That long, measuring look. Then he got into the other side of the car. The kid started the car, and that big beautiful car slid off into the dark night, down the highway. Their headlights were still off.

"What was that?" I said. Cal Meade didn't answer for a minute. Then he said, "Trouble."

FIFTEEN

MABEL ENTRINGER

Saturday morning was cool and fresh. Usually I'd stay home on a Saturday. Between school during the week and church on Sunday, Saturday was the only morning I could rest. I could wash clothes, clean house, and maybe read a book. With that little cool and fresh breeze blowing out of the north, I suddenly felt like taking a walk around town. I had no plan or reason for going. I just wanted to start walking around to see the sights.

I missed that about Excelsior Springs. It was such a pretty town, and we had some big hotels. They lit up in the evening with a soft glow. You could see white folks inside the first floor windows, enjoying their dinners. There were a few Negro hotels, too. We had parks, and sidewalks, and shops, and cafes. There were plenty of places to sit outside or walk, and see townspeople and hotel guests in their nice clothes, going about their day.

Wellington was no Excelsior Springs. Wellington had a few brick streets that kept the dust down. We had businesses and shops. We had a courthouse square with a few trees. Last year, someone built a bench under one of those trees. As long as a white person didn't want to sit there, any colored person in Wellington could enjoy a rest.

Feeling fresh and ready for the day, I walked around downtown Wellington. I wore my yellow dress and my big hat. I carried my flowered cloth bag. I might find something to take to school to feed the children. Someone might give me some apples, or I might find some cans of beans on sale. Once, Mr. Sayed, the owner of Sayed's Department store, gave me two jars of honey! His family in the country of Jordan had just sent him some. The honey was dark, and had an unusual taste. It was deeply sweet in a way I cannot explain. Our American honey was light in color. It was sweet, too, but somehow American honey disappeared from the tongue quickly. It melted away in the mouth. Mr. Sayed's honey stayed like a thick delicious candy. The children loved it.

I had some luck right away. I stopped at Aunt Ida's café for coffee. This was the only place in town Negroes could get a meal or a cup of coffee. Aunt Ida's was on a back street, one that swam in deep dust. I brushed my black-now-dust-red-brown shoes off before I went into the café. The restaurant kept a small broom just outside the door. I walked into the small bright place and saw some people I knew. Essie Fornum was there, and Mae Morris. I said hello to both of them, and sat down by myself at table near the front. I enjoyed a cup of coffee with lots of fresh cream in it. While I drank my coffee, Aunt Ida herself came from the back. She carried two dozen fresh eggs in two cloth bags! She said, "My sister's visiting from Oklahoma. They got rain there— lots of rain. She brought five dozen eggs! Her flock is doing so well. You take some for the Booker T. Washington School."

"What?" I said. "That's too much. Your customers will eat these in no time."

"Nah," Aunt Ida said. "I meant to give you some greens last month and maybe a ham, but business is off. Folks don't have money right now. It used to be that folks would buy a fried chicken dinner. Now, they just want to have soup, or coffee, or plain bread. Anything cheap that fills their stomachs. I had to use that ham to make one week's worth of bean soup."

I couldn't say anything. Finally I said, "Well, you make delicious soup."

Aunt Ida went on like I hadn't spoken. "My garden greens just aren't growing like they should. No rain here." She handed me the two bags of eggs. She walked back to her kitchen. The door closed and I heard her yelling at the kitchen help, "Where are you taking those potatoes?!"

I paid for my coffee. At five cents, it was still the best in town, although white people never had coffee here. "They are missing out," I thought.

I was not trying to go anywhere special today, but I had a sudden thought. I wanted to visit my friend Marian Hodges. I wanted to see how her boy James was doing. Then I could walk a little more to the Booker T. Washington School, find a cool spot in our kitchen, and leave the two bags of beautiful eggs from Oklahoma. I left Aunt Ida's and started my walk to the Hodges'.

SIXTEEN

MABEL ENTRINGER

When I arrived at Marian Hodges' house, I thought at first no one was home. I knocked at the front door. No one answered. I heard voices in the back yard.

"That has to be Caitlin," I thought. No one else could talk so much, so fast. I couldn't hear clearly, but the slower sweet voice had to be Marian's. She was doing her best to answer Caitlin's endless questions.

I walked around to the back of the house. The yard was bare dirt with a few patches of brown grass. I found Marian hanging out laundry. I heard her say, "I don't know when it's going to rain," and then "Mabel might come. Why don't you check out at the front gate?" Just as she said that, she saw me. She smiled her sweet smile, and then she looked at her house.

Caitlin was standing under a second-story window. She was looking up. A dirty white string hung down from the window. The window was open and empty. Or was it? As I watched, Caitlin reached down to a pile of things on the ground. She picked up a small object. Then she tied the object with the string and gave the string a hard pull. Within seconds, the object—what was it? A small box?—was pulled up by some unseen hand. I heard a child cough and then laugh. James must be feeling better. I heard Marian laugh, too. Then Caitlin saw me.

"Mabel!" she said, running over to me.

"Hello Caitlin," I said. "What's going on here? Some sort of secret delivery?"

As Caitlin always did, she answered seriously. She had not noticed my little joke. "Mother says I can't see James yet. He's still sick."

I nodded and said, "Uh-hum."

"She said as long as I send things *up* but don't touch anything sent *down*, I'll be okay." Caitlin wrinkled her nose. She looked at her mother.

"There's no point in wrinkling your nose, Caitlin," Marian Hodges said. "Do you want the wrinkles to get stuck?"

Caitlin's hand flew to her nose. Then Marian said to me, "James is better. He ate a little this morning. Your chicken soup did the trick."

"Did you try what I said? Having him push his foot against your hand?" I asked.

"Yes," Marian said. "His legs seem pretty strong to me! We made a game of it."

"That is very good indeed!" I said. It was. Someone who couldn't move their legs after such a high fever might have polio. Doctors could do nothing about that.

We talked about things for a few minutes. Marian went to the house for more laundry. Caitlin, of course, started talking again. She wanted to know what I was doing today. I told her I was walking around with no real plan. She wanted to know if downtown was busy. I told her it was not. She wanted to know what coffee tasted like. I told her she would find out when she was older. She wanted to know what was in the two bags I carried. I told her about Aunt Ida's present of two dozen eggs, and that these eggs were from Oklahoma.

"Eggs from Oklahoma?" Caitlin said. Her eyes grew round, like large coat buttons. We looked at the two dozen eggs together. Some were white, some were a beautiful brown, and two were a light blue.

"How do eggs get blue?" She asked. I laughed and explained how some eggs were blue and some were even green. It depended on what the chicken was eating.

I walked over to look at the pile of objects Caitlin was planning to send up to James. Caitlin called up to James to send the string back down. "Okay," I heard him say through the open window. The string came down.

Caitlin had an interesting collection. I saw an empty Veedol oil can, a box of Jello mix, a bar of bath soap (with dirt all over it from being on the ground), a large round box of Quaker oats, a tin of Daydream face powder, and an old Nash's fashion magazine dated September 1930.

It wasn't until Caitlin picked up the bar of bath soap to tie it to the string that a small thought pulled at me. Some memory stirred far back in my head. What was it? Then I had it. Every single object in the pile was bright blue. The Veedol oil can was blue, the Jello box was blue, and the soap was blue.

I asked Caitlin, "Caitlin, honey, why are all these things blue?"

Caitlin answered, "Oh I just miss that blue ball. After all those days seeing it around town, Teddy Rangle found it, picked it up, and took it home on his pa's horse."

Of course, I thought. She's seen the same blue ball I saw

on the way to school. "Well that ball just likes to get around, doesn't it?" I said.

"Did you see it, too?" Caitlin asked.

"Oh, yes," I said. "But then it rolled off."

"Well, Teddy Rangle has it now," Caitlin said.

SEVENTEEN

MARIAN HODGES

Laundry day isn't my favorite day. The clothes, sheets, and towels are heavy. Washing, rinsing, drying, folding, and ironing takes all day. I wash by hand. I rinse by hand. Then, I have to put the clothes through a roller and hang everything out to dry. After a few hours, I take the clothes, sheets, and towels down. Then, I start folding and ironing.

If I had to do laundry, though, today wasn't a bad day for it. It was 10 in the morning—still fresh and cool. By the way the clothes moved on the clotheslines, I guessed the wind was coming from the north. That meant a change in the weather. Would it rain? I hoped so. Everyone hoped so.

When I came out of the house with the last load of towels, I could see Mabel getting ready to leave. She waved and said, "'Bye Marian!" I waved back and watched as she walked around the house and then continued up the street toward the Booker T. Washington School. I watched until her yellow dress was just a spot of color in the dusty red distance. I loved that dress. It made Mabel's brown eyes glow. Then I looked over at what Caitlin was doing. A blue box of Quaker oats was going up to James' room on the dirty white string.

"Caitlin!" I called out.

"Yes?" Caitlin was watching the Quaker oats box disappear into James' open window. James said something I couldn't hear.

"What?" Caitlin asked James.

Caitlin didn't see me as I sneaked up behind her. Then I saw my blue tin of Daydream face powder on the ground. I quietly picked it up, opened it, and put some powder on my finger. When Caitlin turned around, I was right behind her. Before she could do anything, I put the white powder on her nose.

"Mother!" she yelled. She jumped away and wiped at her nose, laughing. "How do you do that? How do you always sneak up on me like that?"

"When you come back after putting all these things away —*where they are supposed to go*—I'll tell you." I said. I handed her the Jello box, the Veedol oil can, and my tin of Daydream face powder. Caitlin ran off, into the house. I hoped she was putting everything away.

I felt another cool breeze from the north. My little backyard trees moved. Their leaves rustled. The sound made me think of evening. I loved evenings, when all the work was done. I could be still and think. I walked over to the backyard water pump and filled the bucket with water. Then I went over to one of my trees, and poured water slowly onto the dirt, down into the roots of the tree.

"Mother?" came a voice from the second story window.

"Yes James?" I said, as I went to the backyard water pump to get more water for the bucket.

"When can I come downstairs?" James asked. "I'm tired of staying in this room."

I laughed. "Then you must be feeling better," I said.

"Uh-huh," James said.

"How about tonight for dinner, then?" I asked.

"Okay," James said.

I looked up at my boy. He was leaning out his window. His hair stood straight up, from being in bed. He looked over my trees toward downtown. He asked, "Is there a circus coming to town?"

"A circus?" I said. "What made you think of a circus?"

"I don't know," he said. "I just thought a circus would be fun." He disappeared back into his room. In a few minutes, I saw two bare white feet stick out the window a little. He was sitting in a chair and resting his feet on the windowsill.

I decided to ask Caitlin to run to her father's newspaper office. If Tom could come home a little early, we could have dinner, and then take a walk in the evening around town. Wearing our best clothes, walking in cool blue evening light, gave me such peace. Maybe, for the first time, Caitlin could watch James by herself.

EIGHTEEN

TOM HODGES

Business at the newspaper office was really slow. I didn't expect Bill or Cal to come to work. It was a good day to clean up the newspaper press and get ready for the following work week. Downtown Wellington was completely quiet. Even that Saturday, June 10, it was empty. That was strange. Usually a town like Wellington filled up on Saturdays. People came from all over the county to shop and get something to eat. They sat on their horses, or their wagons, or their trucks, and talked over all their news, like who was getting married, or who had a baby. They might talk about who was visiting from Dallas, or who was starting a new "Home Demonstration" club. Some would talk about how their cotton crop was doing, what price farmers down south got for cotton last year, or how their cattle and pigs were doing. People who came to town always had news.

It was cool today, however, so maybe people wanted to rest and stay home. Some had to ride their horses from nine or ten miles away. That trip would take two hours, at least. A truck might not be much faster. Most of our roads were made of dirt, and no one wanted to risk getting a flat tire. No one had money to replace a flat tire. You had to go slow and be careful about your tires.

Caitlin came by with lunch in a small tin bucket. Marian packed a good lunch. She made a meatloaf sandwich with pickles. I pulled a jar of cold iced tea from the bucket and gave some to Caitlin to drink. She always stayed while I ate. Then she took the lunch bucket back to Marian. Today, she said, "Mother wants you to come home. She's making an early dinner."

"Oh yes?" I asked.

"Uh-huh!" Caitlin said. "James is coming downstairs for dinner!"

"Oh," I said. "That's good, then."

It *was* good news. Maybe James had a bad cold or something like that. Marian's mother says that summer colds are the worst.

I didn't have much to do after lunch. I opened the front and back doors to let the cool breeze through. I sat down and made some notes on a new story I wanted to write. You could read any newspaper in Texas, or in America for that matter, and they said the same thing: we should be brave. We should be patient and hang on. We need to make do with less. We needed to trust our leaders to do the right things.

I wanted to write something new. What were people really thinking about? Did they think better times would come? What did they think would happen to them? What if better times did not come?

Many of us were new to Wellington. We came from Oklahoma, Missouri, Iowa, or other parts of Texas. Some even came from outside the United States. We could leave and go somewhere else.

Other Wellington families had been here for thirty years or more. They spent a good part of their lives and their money to live here. They built their farms and homes and businesses over many years. Did they think they had made a mistake? It seemed to me they faced the same question all of us did. Will you stay here or will you go away?

Just before I left for home, Cal Meade stopped by the office. He said that he had a one-hour job that paid good money. He would share the job with me if we could use my truck. I asked him what the job was.

"I got a load of ice and food for that tourist motel out there north of town," Cal said.

"You mean that place north of here on the highway? About six miles away, on the river?" I asked.

"That's the one," Cal said. "The owner's got a new restaurant up there to go with his little motel."

"A new restaurant, huh?" I asked. "I know the place. I can go in an hour."

"Pick me up at five o'clock at Olsen's Ice House," he said.

I closed up the office and walked home.

NINETEEN

MARIAN HODGES

When Tom got home, he told me about the job. Cal Meade needed his help taking some ice and food out someplace north of town. He'd be back in one or two hours.

"All right," I said. "It's four o'clock now. We can have dinner early. When you get back, I want us to dress up and walk around town."

"What?" Tom asked.

"You heard me!" I said.

Tom laughed. "I can't think of anything I'd rather do than walk around town with a beautiful lady."

Caitlin and I put dinner on the table quickly. We had more of the meatloaf I made, green beans, and biscuits. James came downstairs. His dark hair stuck straight up. His clothes looked too big. He was pale and wobbly. He used both his little hands to hold onto his glass of milk. He didn't eat too much. After five days in bed, that wasn't a surprise.

After dinner, I planned to heat some water and give him a bath. Caitlin could take a bath, too. I could change into my best green dress. When Tom got back home, we'd go for a walk downtown.

It was no surprise that Caitlin was unhappy about my plan. "Mother!" said Caitlin. "I don't want a bath!" She moved closer to the back door. Somehow, Caitlin hated to get her hair wet. I never knew why. She was like that since she was a baby.

"You're not going anywhere, daughter of mine." Then I thought, and said, "I have that blue bath soap. The soap you keep taking? Have you ever smelled it? It smells good, like flowers or a tree in spring. You can take a bath with that."

Caitlin looked a little happier. I sighed. I knew I would have to pour water over her head to wash her hair. She wouldn't do it. I got our big milk pitcher out of the kitchen to do the pouring. 大水壶

TWENTY

TOM HODGES

The sun was still up at five o'clock. It was starting to look orange. It dropped closer to the dusty fields in the west.

When I got to Olsen's Ice House, Cal Meade was waiting for me. My truck was an old flatbed Ford—the farmer's favorite truck. You could put almost anything on it. Tonight, we shoveled sawdust into the bed of the truck. I needed about two inches of it to keep the ice off of the truck's hot wood bed. The ice wouldn't melt that way.

Mickey Olsen gave us a few shovels and pointed to a pile of sawdust inside the ice house. The sawdust was light and fluffy. It smelled like the trees and woods it came from— maybe from Oklahoma or Arkansas. Working together, we didn't take long to put a few inches in the truck. Olsen's men dragged two big blocks of ice out and put them on the sawdust.

Cal already had the food the motel owner wanted. He tucked the bag with the food between the two ice blocks. We got the shovels again. The ice needed a few more inches of saw dust on the top to keep it cool. We had to drive six miles.

Even though there was a cool north breeze today, the ice would start melting quickly if we didn't take care. I threw a canvas sheet over everything and tied it down. It should be all right.

Cal and I got into the truck and drove out to the highway. I turned left at Highway 83 from 8th Street and started down the empty road. As we passed the D.C.D. #2 gas station on our left, Cal moved and made a little sound.

"What is it?" I asked.

Cal was looking past me through my open window. I slowed down and looked where he was looking. I saw a very large and fancy dark red V8 Ford at the gas pump. The driver was getting gas. He was a well-dressed man in a white shirt. He was not very tall. I had an idea a few people were with him, waiting in the car. I don't know why I thought that. I was driving, and I didn't have much time to see inside his car.

Cal finally said, "I saw them last night on the newspaper delivery."

"Oh?" I asked. Cal didn't say anything. Finally, I said, "Nice car. We don't see those big V8s too often." There was another long pause.

"Right," Cal said. Then I heard his stomach growl. I laughed.

I said, "Feeling hungry Cal?"

"Yes," Cal said.

"We'll be home soon," I said.

The tourist motel wasn't too far, but my load was heavy so I couldn't drive fast. We sent up big long rivers of dust behind us. Cal looked back a few times. I didn't know what he was looking for. With all that dust, surely he couldn't see anything much.

The miles went by...three...four...five. We saw a few

houses set back from the highway. Each house had small trees. I thought of my wife, Marian, who watered our poor little backyard trees.

With just one mile to go, we were at the bottom of a long, gentle hill going up. Once we got to the top of the hill, we'd be able to see the whole valley formed by the Salt Fork of the Red River. The tourist motel would be right at the bottom, just on the other side of the old bridge. It was starting to get dark. You could just see the top of the red blazing sun in the west. The little engine on my old Ford truck got louder as we took the hill. I shifted down to second gear. The ice blocks were heavy.

About halfway up, we heard a horn honking. It was so loud I thought at first it was a train, but that made no sense. The train line was far from here. I heard it again. This time it was right behind us.

Cal and I jumped. I looked in the rearview mirror, but all I could see was a thick cloud of dust. Some bright headlights came on, and the horn honked again. Something came out of the dust cloud. It was the dark red Ford V8 coming up behind us. It was moving so fast I could hardly believe it. What was the driver doing? Was he out of his mind? Was he trying to kill us or kill himself?

I pulled over to the right as far as I could. I'd let that crazy driver go around me. But the Ford V8 stayed right behind us. It looked like he'd hit my truck. That horn honked again. Cal's eyes were wide open.

I felt my right wheels edge off the road. We got thrown to the right. This was not good. I thought we would hit a rock or flip over. But at the last minute, the big Ford V8 went around on our left. As it roared ahead of us, it knocked my side mirror off.

"Hey!" I shouted. My engine stalled and the truck stopped. Cal and I sat, breathing hard. We couldn't talk. That was close! The dust cloud slowly drifted down around us.

I caught my breath and said, "What was *that*?"

Cal said, "Bad luck."

"Well," I said. "If that was bad luck, it's gone around us."

Cal shook his head. "No," he said.

TWENTY-ONE

TOM HODGES

I got out of my truck and walked back on the road to find my side mirror. Maybe I could save it. I didn't have money to replace it. I found it, but it was smashed. I threw it off the road. I picked up a few larger pieces of the broken glass, and threw those off the road, too.

Cal got out and looked over my tires. Then he checked the ice blocks and the food. "Everything looks fine," he said.

"All right," I said. "Let's see if I can it started." Luckily, the truck started up. I didn't want to be stuck out here with night coming soon. I slowly drove the truck back onto the highway. Just when I thought everything was all right, the truck engine stalled again.

"Oh come on," I said. I tried to start the truck, but it was no good. The engine just went *whir whir whir*, but it didn't start.

"Just wait a minute," Cal said. "See if it just needs time."

"All right," I said. As we waited, it got darker.

"Let's try one more time," I said. The truck started. I hoped it would keep running. We'd already lost twenty minutes. I told Marian it would only take me an hour or two. We'd been gone over two hours.

A few minutes later, we saw the river valley below us. A few lights down at the tourist motel had come on. The lights were a clear yellow in the soft blue darkness.

"Look there," Cal said. He pointed.

Just west of the motel, on our side of the river, we saw a few tiny lights. They weren't electric. We could barely see them. They looked like old fashioned lanterns. Cal's night vision was good. I might not have seen them.

"Huh," I said. "That's the Rangle's land. Maybe someone's fishing down there, or taking a swim. It's a nice evening for it."

"It sure is," Cal said. His stomach growled again.

"Not much longer," I said. We started down the long slope to the river.

"Careful about that bridge," Cal said.

"Yeah," I said. The bridge across the river was closed for repairs. I had to make a detour to the right. This meant getting off the highway and going far downstream. Then I had to go down the steep riverbank. The road engineers made a stone ford through the river down at the bottom. I could drive through the river, and it was just a few inches deep. Mostly, we wouldn't get stuck in the mud. The Salt Fork of the Red River actually had water and mud in it. In this part of Texas, a lot of other rivers go dry in summer. That's the way this place was—not having any rain didn't help.

I got over the river ford, and got my truck up the riverbank on the far side. The river made a quiet laughing sound. There were trees. The air smelled good, like water and living things. I looked at the Rangle place, but didn't see the lantern lights anymore. The Rangles must have gone home.

The tourist motel was just a minute farther on the highway. The little parking lot had four or five cars in it. That surprised me. I didn't know anyone would come all the way out here just for dinner. They must be travelers. Maybe they were staying at the tourist motel overnight. I wondered if Marian would like to come out here. We could get something to eat at the new restaurant and maybe walk down to the river after.

The owner of the tourist motel said he'd given up on us. "I've got a restaurant full of guests. They are ready to eat. Some folks are from Dallas," he said.

"We had a little trouble on the way, but we made it. We got all you asked for," Cal said.

"Ten pounds of hamburger?" the man asked.

"Yes sir," Cal said.

The owner, was a short, thick-bodied, red-haired man named Carter. He took the bag of food. He practically ran into the restaurant. I heard him yelling at his kitchen help, "Here we go!" There was a shout of laughter. Two of his men, one Negro and one white, came out to get the ice blocks. They had a small cart. We loaded one block on, and the two men went back inside the kitchen. It was slow. That ice block was heavy.

Cal and I waited. I walked to the edge of the parking lot. I stood in the grass away from the light of the restaurant. It was completely dark out by the river. The grass here was soft and green. I saw those weak lantern lights again. There was one, then two, and then three. They were on the far side of the river, over at the Rangle place. It looked like they were moving away, like someone came to the river a second time, and then changed their minds and went back home. Cal came over to watch with me.

The kitchen help came back for the second ice block. Carter followed them. He was carrying two plates of food.

"Hey, now," he said. "Have some dinner. It's on me. It's the least I can do. You really saved the day!"

"Oh," I said. "No, thanks, that's..." and then I stopped. Cal stared at the dinner plates. I then understood that Cal Meade was very hungry. Why didn't I see that? He told me he was hungry. I thought he just meant he was hungry for dinner. Now I thought Cal had not had breakfast or lunch either. I was angry at myself. It's true Cal was strong, but he was looking thin, too. He probably wasn't making much money out at the Booker T. Washington School. He probably got a lot less than I did at the newspaper, too. That wasn't much money at all.

"That'll be fine," I said, quickly. "It looks great."

"Thank you," Cal said.

"When you're finished, let me know. I'll pay you then," said Carter. He went back into his brightly lit restaurant.

light 的处于状

TWENTY-TWO

TEDDY RANGLE

It turned out to be an exciting day. I'll never forget it. Ma still starts to cry whenever we talk about it. Pa shakes his head, and then we go outside. We talk about that Saturday without Ma hearing. I had so many questions. Who were those people in the fancy red car? How did they miss the bridge detour sign? I wonder what they thought when their fancy car ended up in the river mud? That must have been a surprise. Why did those men leave the lady in the car? Where did they get all those guns?

"Pa," I asked, "How did you know those people were trouble?"

Pa answered, "They wouldn't tell us their names."

That was true. It all started when those two guys came to the house. They said they crashed their car into the river and that they needed help. Pa and my big brother Lance talked to them. Lance had a new pickup truck from his oil job in Pampa. He thought he could use his truck to get their car out of the river. The water was only six inches deep. Then Pa told him they ought to walk down to the car first to see what was going on. By this time, it was completely dark. Pa told me to get our old lanterns out. I ran and got them. Pa lit them, and gave one of them to the man who was doing most of the talking. Was he the car's driver?

I got a chance to look both guys over. One was young—kind of rough looking. He looked scared. His eyes kept moving around and his hands were shaking. He hardly said a word. The other man was older. He had dark eyes. He wasn't tall. He had blood on his nice white shirt. His dark hair was messy. He said he'd been thrown from the car. When he saw me looking at him, I looked away fast. He didn't seem mad. He just looked sort of cold, like an older kid at school you knew you were going to get in a fight with.

We all went down to the river. We found their car. It was a big car, and it was nose down in the mud. The rear tires were up on the riverbank. I could smell something strange, like gas or oil. It was a burning smell, but I couldn't see a fire.

Pa said to the older man, 'You must have missed the bridge detour sign." The man didn't answer. He didn't even look at Pa. He just walked past the car and into the darkness. We heard him open the back door of the car.

"Come help me W.D.!" he called out. The young scared guy ran around to help. In a few minutes, he came back with five or six long, dark objects. Were those *guns*? Pa and Lance looked at each other. The young kid put the guns on the ground, and then went around to other side of the car again. Pa said something quiet to Lance. I heard Lance say "Okay."

We heard someone crying. A high voice said, "Help! Get me out of here!" It was from inside the car. Pa and Lance ran to the car door closest to us. Pa gave me his lantern.

He said, "There's a kid in there, or a woman!" He opened the car door and put his hand through. He could barely see the older man's white shirt on the other side of the car, taking more guns out. That burning smell was getting stronger.

"Pa!" I said. "Something smells bad."

Pa said, "Why didn't you tell us someone was in the car? Help me!" The man didn't answer. He called out to the young kid, "W.D.! Go help him over there! Get her out!"

The young guy, "W.D.," I guess his name was, ran back around the car. He looked more scared than before. He was only 16 or 17. Together, W.D. and Pa got a tiny woman out of the car. She was young. I caught a flash of dark blonde hair in the lantern light. She couldn't stand up. Pa put her on the ground. I held the lantern up high. Pa and I gasped. The bad smell was coming from her. Her whole right side was wet with something. From the smell, and her crying, you could see it wasn't water. Something from the car? I looked around for Lance, but I didn't see him.

"Pa!" I asked. "Where's Lance?"

Pa put his fingers to his lips, "Shh...," he said. He looked over at the car. He pulled me over close. Then he said, quietly, "I sent Lance to town to get help. Something's wrong here. Now hush up."

I hushed up.

The two men came back around to our side of the car. W.D. carried eight or nine shotguns and rifles. He was having a hard time carrying those guns. I'd never seen so many guns together, except when Pa took me to visit Sheriff Black at the jail last year. All the guns there had been locked up behind glass. They were only for the Sheriff and his deputies to use.

The older man was carrying a large bag. It looked heavy. He came over to where the woman lay on the ground. His white shirt now had dirt marks on it as well as blood.

Pa said, "She's hurt bad. She needs a doctor."

The man said, "We're not calling a doctor. Let's take her up to your place. Maybe there's something you can do for her there."

I thought Pa would argue. But he didn't. The man and W.D. carried the guns back up to our house. Pa and I tried to help the lady stand up, but she still couldn't stand. Pa picked her up and carried her. He told me later she was light, like a child. He was careful not to touch the side where her clothes were wet. I carried the lantern.

We were walking off into the darkness. We had no idea who these people were, or what they wanted.

TWENTY-THREE

TEDDY RANGLE

put out 爆死 体到关扑灭消衰

We got back to the house. Ma and my sister-in-law, Lulu, met us at the door. Lulu was carrying little Sybil, my baby niece. Sybil had been crying all day. The only thing that helped was Ma or Lulu carrying her.

Ma came out on the front porch. "What's going on?" she asked. She looked worried. She saw the two men and all those guns. Pa put the lady on the porch. She'd stopped crying. Now she just shivered.

"This lady is hurt, Myrtle," Pa said. "See what you can do. Start by getting a blanket. Did Lance go to town?"

"Yeah, he went," Lulu said from inside the front door. "He wouldn't tell us anything." She sounded put out. Lulu was a pretty girl. My brother Lance loved her, but Lulu's voice was high and loud. Her big voice didn't match her pretty face. Tonight, of course, the older man heard what she said.

He said, "Where's that truck I saw earlier?"

Pa answered, "I sent my son to town to get help."

"What?" the older man said. Now he sounded almost

angry. "I don't want that. No ambulance, no doctor." He looked at my Pa, hard.

Pa said, "He's going to get a larger truck to get your car out of the river. That's what I told him." He turned to Lulu and said, "Honey, take little Sybil inside. Go help Myrtle find a blanket for this lady." Lulu made a sour face, but she went.

"All right," the older man said. He seemed to relax. He sat down on one of our porch chairs. He looked off into the darkness toward the river. "I don't know how it happened," he said.

"How what happened?" Pa asked.

"How I missed that bridge," the man said.

W.D. spoke up. He was just a shape in the darkness. "I saw what happened. It was that blue ball, or something blue. It rolled across the road where you should have taken that detour."

"I didn't see a blue ball," the older man said.

"Sure, it was there. Like a kid's play ball, or something. It was like a basketball, but blue," said W.D. "Your headlights were shining on it, and you looked over at it for just a second. That was long enough to miss the detour sign, I guess."

The older man stood up. He sounded tired. "Well," he said, "that makes no sense at all. It's just bad luck."

A blue ball? I thought. I only knew of one blue ball—my blue ball. Well, it was almost mine. It was the one I'd picked up in town the other day. It was soft and bouncy. I could bounce it against my bedroom wall and Ma and Pa wouldn't hear it. I went inside the house and ran up to my room. Of course, the ball wasn't there. Where did it go? Out of our house, and then across Highway 83, I guess. The day was already so strange. I laughed.

I went downstairs and out on the porch. Ma was getting

the lady's clothes off. Her dress tore like wet pieces of paper. "What in the world?" Ma asked.

Pa said, quietly, "I think that's battery acid, or something from the car. Maybe the battery broke open when they crashed. It's burned her and smells bad. Make sure you wash your hands when you're done there. It might burn you, too."

Ma washed the woman off with warm water and covered her with the blanket. "There's not much more I can do here."

The man and the young kid stood off in the darkness, talking quietly. I couldn't hear what they said.

Ma leaned over the lady, and said to her, "You should drink some water. I'll go get some."

The lady sat up a little. She held the blanket around her shoulders. She looked at me, Pa, and Ma, and said, clearly, "I want a cigarette."

TWENTY-FOUR

TOM HODGES

The dinner Carter brought out for us was good. The cook at his restaurant was good. We each had a piece of roast chicken, some mashed carrots and potatoes, and fried mustard greens. It was a good Southern meal.

Cal said, "I know only one person who makes mustard greens like this—Mabel Entringer. She has a lot of them in her garden."

"Hmm," I said, in between mouthfuls of mashed carrots and the peppery, buttery greens. I handed my roast chicken leg to Cal. I told him, "I already ate before I picked you up. Take it."

Without argument, Cal took the roast chicken leg. He ate the juicy meat off the bone. The chicken skin was crispy and golden. Even though he was hungry, Cal didn't hurry. He wanted to enjoy the food as long as he could.

We sat together in the darkness at the edge of the parking lot. It was a quiet night. If you listened hard you could hear the river. We heard night insects, and the lonely call of a night bird in the trees. We heard the restaurant customers talking and laughing inside.

Cal touched my arm. "Look there," he said.

I looked across the river and saw some car lights. There were lights from a truck, too. They moved slowly from Highway 83 toward the Rangle place.

"That's Sheriff Black's car," Cal said. "I don't know whose truck that is."

I was impressed Cal could see that well, and that he knew the owner of a car by looking at it. I probably should talk to Cal if I wanted good background information for my newspaper stories. I started to ask Cal what he thought about the hard times we were having in Wellington, but just then the restaurant owner, Carter, came out to pay us, and take his plates. He gave us each $7, which was more than I expected.

"It's for all the trouble you had getting here," Carter said.

We both thanked him. Then Cal asked, "Mr. Carter, have you got Mabel Entringer working in your kitchen?"

Carter blinked. "Mabel Entringer? No, but I tried to hire her. She gave me the name of a student of hers at the colored school over in Wellington—Missy Derby. I hired her. She's a good cook. Those mustard greens come from Mabel's garden. She's the only one who has fresh vegetables growing for miles around."

Carter said goodnight and went back inside his restaurant. I was thinking we should go home when I heard a man yell. It was across the river.

"Halt!" the voice shouted. Then again, "Halt! Stop right there!" Then we heard a gunshot. A woman screamed. Then we heard two more shots, and then another.

Cal and I looked at each other. We ran to the truck. Something bad was happening at the Rangles'. My bad luck was back! My truck would not start. *Whir whir whir,* went the engine again. Carter came out of his restaurant.

"Was that a gun shot?" he asked.

"Yes," I said. "It sounded like it." I was still trying to start my truck.

"Leave it," Cal said. "Let's just run over. The river is low. We can wade across it."

"Have you got a phone?" I asked Carter.

"Sure," he said.

"Call Sheriff Black."

As Cal and I ran to the river, I knew Sheriff Black wouldn't answer the phone. He was already at the Rangles' place, if Cal saw correctly. I thought he probably did.

We got down to the river. We could just wade through it. It wasn't deep. As we were starting to cross, we heard a car start. We heard more yelling, this time a woman, "Ow! Stop pulling on me! It hurts!" Then a man screamed, "Get in! Let's go! Move it!"

What was going on over there?

The river was deeper than we thought. It took us a few minutes to get across. By then, we heard the car leaving. It was headed for Highway 83. We both looked down the river to the bridge detour. Sure enough, in just a minute, we saw a car drive across the stone ford, and up the other riverbank. The car was headed away from Wellington to the north. Its engine made a high whine.

"Sheriff Black's car again," Cal said. "He's going the wrong way."

We climbed up the steep riverbank. I ran into something. Something really large. "What in the world?" I said.

"It's a car," Cal said.

"What?" I said.

"It's that fancy red Ford V8. It's empty," Cal said. "How'd it get down here?"

Cal's eyes were much better than mine. He went in front of me. We had to get to the Rangles' to see if they were all right. It was only a few minutes away.

We walked fast.

TWENTY-FIVE

TOM HODGES

We got to the Rangles' house to find a mess. It was an old-fashioned ranch house. They didn't have electricity. We found the house because they had lanterns burning on their porch. We found Mr. Rangle and his son Lance looking at two flat tires on their truck.

"I've only got one spare tire," Lance said. "Even if we could change the tires, they're moving too fast for us. We'll never catch them."

We walked up, out of the darkness, and both men jumped. "It's just me and Cal Meade," I said. "We were over at the tourist motel. Is everyone all right?"

Everyone was *not* all right. We found Mrs. Myrtle Rangle trying to help a young woman in the kitchen by lantern light. She was crying as Mrs. Rangle poured water over her bleeding hand. I saw Teddy Rangle, the younger son, holding a crying baby in his arms. He was standing in the corner of the kitchen. He rocked the baby, but it didn't help. The baby was screaming at the top of her lungs. Teddy went "Shh, shh, shh," trying to quiet the child.

"What happened?" I asked.

Mrs. Rangle said, "Those people! They were outside. Lulu tried to lock the screen door so they couldn't come back into the house. They shot her through the door while she was holding the baby!"

I couldn't make much sense of what Mrs. Rangle was saying. From the other family members, I put together a very strange story. Two men had come to the house. One of them was young and scared looking. The other one was older and well-dressed. They'd missed the bridge detour and wrecked their car in the river. Mr. Rangle and his son had gone to help. They found a badly burned woman in the car. They brought her back to the house. This part was clear.

Then, the story got really strange. The car was full of guns. The two men were acting strangely, and wouldn't say their names. They wouldn't go for a doctor.

The Rangle men were excited to tell the story. They were talking at the same time. Teddy Rangle said, "Well, that young kid was named 'W.D.' That's what the older man called him."

Then Lance went into town to get Sheriff Black. Mr. Rangle said, "I told those guys a story about getting a bigger truck to get their car out of the river. I knew they were trouble, and I secretly told Lance to get the Sheriff."

"I found the Sheriff, and I brought him back to the house," Lance said.

"The next thing we knew, something set one of them off," Mr. Rangle said.

"The older one," Teddy Rangle said. "He was like a madman."

Lance Rangle said, "He pulled out one of his guns and shot at the house. Then he grabbed Sheriff Black and pushed him into the Sheriff's car. He shot out my truck's tires so we couldn't drive away. The young guy picked up the burned woman and took her to the car, too. They left all her clothes."

"Then they drove off," Mr. Rangle said.

I was starting to get an idea of who these visitors were. I said, "We saw the car driving to the north."

Mr. Rangle said, "We need to get to a phone. Call the sheriff in Pampa, north of here. We've got to call someone!"

I told Mr. Rangle that Carter, the restaurant owner, was calling someone. If he couldn't get Sheriff Black on the phone, he might get one of the deputies.

"Did you hear any more of their names when they were talking to each other?" I asked.

"No," Lance said. "We just heard that scary guy call the kid 'W.D.'"

"Did they leave anything behind?" I asked.

Mr. Rangle pushed a pile of ladies' things on the floor with his foot. There was a dress, some shoes, some white gloves, and a cheap cigarette case. One side of the dress was ruined with some kind of liquid. It smelled awful. The guns, the fancy fast car running us off the road, the nice clothes, and the man's willingness to shoot—this was starting to add up.

I did not know that name, "W.D."

However, I was fairly sure the Rangles had just hosted Clyde Barrow and Bonnie Parker.

TWENTY-SIX

MARIAN HODGES

I waited up until ten. Tom still wasn't home. Something must have happened. I couldn't decide if I was worried or angry. I checked on Caitlin and James. They were both asleep in their beds. I touched James' head. He felt a little warm, I thought. I couldn't do anything about it now.

I walked over to our neighbors' house. Frank and Addie Welton had a white house across the street. They had a telephone. I would call Sheriff Black. It was late, and I thought they might be in bed already, but I saw a light in the window. I heard music. I knocked softly on their door.

"We're just listening to a little music on the radio," Addie said. "It helps us get to sleep." She was a tiny woman. Tonight she wore a blue bathrobe. I was used to seeing her in a dress with a matching hat, shoes, and handbag. She was in and out of her house all day, going to meetings or church. She once raised $225 for some farmers in the county who were going to lose their farms to the bank. With all her daily business, and comings and goings, no wonder she had trouble falling asleep.

Addie led me to their front hall and showed me their telephone. When I called Sheriff Black's, the phone just rang and rang. No one answered. I wasn't sure what to do.

Addie must have seen the worry on my face. Her large blue eyes looked me over. She said, "What's going on Marian? Is everything all right?"

"I don't know," I said. "Tom is hours late. I expected him back long ago. He had a job driving some ice and food up to the tourist motel north of town. I tried to call Sheriff Black, but no one answers."

"That's a dark road, and there's a bridge detour. Was he with anyone?" Addie asked.

"Cal Meade," I said. "He told Tom about the job."

"Well now," Addie said, "Cal Meade's a good man. No one knows the road better. No one can fix a flat tire better. I'm sure that's all it is. They've probably had a flat tire."

Addie tried to make me feel better. It wasn't working. She took the phone from me and hung it up. Then she called to her husband in the other room, "Frank, can you think of any reason why Sheriff Black wouldn't answer his phone?"

"It could be anything," Frank said. He walked into the front hall. He was a large man, yet his step was quiet. He was wearing a white shirt and dark pants. He always wore nice office clothes, even at home. He was a judge at the county courthouse. He knew Sheriff Black well, and saw him every day. He said in his deep voice, "Maybe they got a call, and he had to go. I know he's short one deputy. Bill Ross should have been working tonight, but is sick with a fever. His wife said he was talking crazy. He is sick with that summer cold everyone's been getting."

Addie Welton looked at her husband with her blue eyes. He looked back. A few seconds passed. She was tiny, and he was tall.

Judge Frank Welton said, "Well, I'll just walk over to the courthouse now and see if I can find out what's going on. Maybe I can call another deputy." With that, he put on his hat and left.

I thanked Addie, and told her I had to get back to the children. She said, "I'll send Frank over if he hears anything." She shut her door.

I made my way back to my house across the dry dust of our street. I'd left the front porch light on. Some insects were flying around it the warm, yellow light. I heard a dog bark, far away. There was a slight breeze from the east. The wind had shifted again. I decided to stay outside for a few minutes. Maybe I would see Tom's truck any minute. I breathed in.

Then I jumped. A tiny little hand touched my arm. "Boo," my daughter Caitlin said.

"Ahhh!" I screamed. I overdid my scream, just a little. She surprised me, but I wasn't scared by it.

"I got you," Caitlin said.

I held her close, and didn't know whether to laugh or cry. She'd finally sneaked up on me.

"What are you doing?" Caitlin asked, after she'd finished giggling.

"Waiting for your father," I said. We just stood together in the cool summer night for a while. Wellington didn't have many streetlights. The town didn't have the money to keep them all on, either. It was nice, in a way. On clear nights we could see the stars. Tonight, far, far off to the east, I thought I saw a storm. It was so far away, over in Oklahoma, that I couldn't be sure. It was just a flicker of light in the sky. Maybe we would get rain soon.

I was just thinking of putting Caitlin to bed when I saw headlights. It was Tom. He pulled into the driveway and turned off the engine. He left the headlights on. Cal Meade was with him. They both had strange looks on their faces, like they'd seen a tornado. The truck was a mess. There was some paint gone on Tom's side. The side mirror was missing.

"What is it?" I asked. "Are you all right?"

Caitlin walked over to the truck. She looked at her father closely. She said, "Something's happened." Neither Tom nor Cal answered.

At just that moment, Judge Frank Welton came into the yard. He was out of breath.

"You will never believe what happened," he said.

"Actually, I probably will," Tom said.

TWENTY-SEVEN

CAITLIN HODGES

Church was interesting that Sunday. After last night, I had a lot of listening to do. Church was a good place to listen, I thought. Mother and Father let me go to a different church every Sunday. A friend from school would invite me, and I would go. I would sit in a church with Jilly Kellerman, her beautiful sisters, and her talkative parents. Sometimes I went with Norma Vinnedge, her little brother, and her pretty mother who was always alone. Annie Foster asked me one week to a new church in someone's living room. They pushed aside the piano and the sofa, and filled the space with a lot of chairs of different sizes. We listened to a radio show, all the way from California. I never knew a church service could be on the radio.

This week I was with Jilly Kellerman. We were at the Grace Lutheran Church on 10th Street. We sat between her two sisters, Katrina and Bettina. The oldest, Katrina, wore a green and white Sunday dress with white shoes and white gloves. Bettina wore pink. That did not surprise me. Bettina was pink all over. With her wavy blond hair and rosy skin, she looked like someone out of a magazine. Sitting between Jilly's sisters was like sitting between tall, soft pink and green flowers in a garden. It was nice.

As the preacher talked on and on, Bettina practiced writing her signature on the white paper of the church program. Each signature got rounder, until the last one she wrote had a tiny heart above the "i" of B-e-t-t-i-n-a.

Katrina was more of a talker. That was perfect for Jilly and me. We could talk quietly throughout the church service. Bettina sat between her parents and us, so they couldn't hear a thing.

"Have you heard?" Katrina whispered.

"Heard what?" Jilly whispered.

"Sheriff Black's missing!" Katrina whispered. "He was taken by a gang with guns. They drove off in the Sheriff's car." Jilly's mouth made a perfect "O."

Of course, I already knew this. Father and Judge Welton talked for a long time last night. After answering a few questions from Judge Welton, Cal Meade got out of the truck, and walked towards the highway. He must have been walking home. I wondered how long he would have to walk, under the stars, through the empty fields.

Judge Welton went into his home and started making phone calls. I thought he must be calling the sheriffs in Pampa, and Childress, and maybe other places. Maybe he was calling the Texas Rangers. They were lawmen who served the entire state of Texas. They would be interested in a Texas sheriff getting kidnapped.

Father came into the house and started making notes. He was writing a story about everything that had happened.

When Mr. Elms, the newspaper owner came back from Dallas, the story would be ready.

I already knew everything Katrina was going to say. Her news was not news to me. I was really interested in how she could talk to us and look like she was just sitting and smiling quietly in church at the same time. That took skill.

Katrina had a few details wrong. Lulu Rangle was not rushed to the hospital with her hand shot off. Father called the hospital before I left the house for church. Lulu was not in the hospital, and she had not been brought there the night before. Father thought that meant Lulu's hand might be all right. If so, Lulu was a lucky lady. Clyde Barrow was not afraid to shoot a gun.

Also, the big red fancy car was not upside down in the river. It did not burn up "in a cloud of black smoke," as Katrina said. Father told Mother he thought the car could be saved. "They could just pull it out of the river. It'll probably drive fine," he said.

After church, everyone stayed longer than usual. Everyone wanted to know the shocking news about the gang who took Sheriff Black and held the Rangle family at gunpoint. No one knew where Sheriff Black was, or if he was all right. "Could it be Bonnie and Clyde?" I heard more than once. Father thought it was Bonnie Parker and Clyde Barrow, and a new gang member named W.D., but he couldn't be sure. He needed more information.

"Caitlin, don't tell anyone it was Bonnie and Clyde. I'm not sure about that yet," he said. I nodded my head. Clearly, from what I heard at church, other people were already thinking that the famous and dangerous Bonnie and Clyde visited Wellington, Texas.

The folks of Grace Lutheran church talked and talked. Jilly

and I had nothing to do but wait until they were done. I told her about the bright blue ball and it how showed up everywhere. It was as blue as a day at the beach. I could never catch it. I told her that Teddy Rangle saw it and picked it up. He took it home on his father's big horse Jacko.

""That's just...wait...what are you trying to say? That some blue ball caused all of this?" Jilly put into words exactly what I was thinking.

"What if it did?" I asked. "What if that blue ball got loose from Teddy and rolled across the road? Maybe it caused Cly- I mean, that driver—to miss the bridge detour?"

Jilly and I got into an argument. She started with, "Balls don't decide to roll away and cause accidents."

I shot back, "The Rangle place is right by that bridge detour."

Jilly was right, of course. But, she hadn't seen that bright blue beach ball. She hadn't seen it show up all over town. She hadn't seen it shiver in the long green grass under the trees. I think that blue ball was on a holiday of its own. It was on a visit. I tried to tell her these things. Even though she laughed at me, it was all right. Jilly and I could argue for hours. We'd still be friends.

The next day, two amazing things happened. It was Monday afternoon during the last week of school. We were sitting on the front steps of the school, waiting for Katrina and Bettina to take Jilly home. I was looking at the sky at dark clouds gathering in the east. I was about to tell Jilly I thought it might rain. Then, out of nowhere, Judge Welton drove up in his black car. He stopped and asked me if Father was at the newspaper office today. I told him he was. Judge Welton thanked me and then said, "Sheriff Black is all right. He was found in Oklahoma, tied to a tree. That gang stole his car. I'm driving over to Oklahoma now to pick him up."

Jilly's eyes grew round. I suppose mine did, too. Judge Welton waved and drove to the highway, towards the newspaper office. As Jilly and I looked at each other and grinned, we heard a deep rumble of thunder.

It started to rain.

TWENTY-EIGHT

CAITLIN HODGES RANGLE

"Reader, I married him."

Ha ha! I got you, didn't I? I still love reading books. That line is from *Jane Eyre*, one of my favorites. That's how the author starts the last chapter. That's how I'll start this chapter. It's the last in this story.

You might ask "Why would little Caitlin Hodges get married? She's only in elementary school." I will get to that. I have a lot to tell. Some of it still seems like it was yesterday.

After Sheriff Black got back home from being kidnapped, he said what everyone had been thinking. On that long, long drive the night of June 10, 1933, the driver told the sheriff he was Clyde Barrow. The woman was Bonnie Parker.

The sheriff told Father he couldn't believe how Bonnie smoked cigarettes, one after the other, even with terrible burns on her leg. Sheriff Black thought for sure they'd kill him. Instead they tied him to a tree and drove away. Bonnie Parker and Clyde Barrow did not live long after that. Less than a year later, in May, 1934 they were shot dead. Six Texas Rangers set a trap along a country road in Louisiana.

They shot the pair over 100 times. They didn't have a chance.

Their beautiful red Ford V8 car was pulled out of the river north of Wellington. As Father had thought, it was fine. It just needed a few repairs. Clyde had stolen it from a doctor in Oklahoma. Someone in Wellington offered to buy it, and the doctor agreed. For the next year or so, we could see that big, beautiful Ford around town.

Our visit from Bonnie and Clyde seemed to start off a lot of changes. The rain we got helped a few farmers get by for a few months. Even Mother's trees started to look good. But, almost every week after that, you heard about a family leaving. People were giving up and moving away. The banks wouldn't lend money. There were too many bad years for cotton and cattle. By the time we left in 1934, I knew at least twenty other families who had gone, too.

Father's newspaper story about Bonnie and Clyde's visit was printed in Dallas, Houston, Oklahoma City, and even in Kansas City and Chicago. The Dallas papers also printed his stories about hard times in Wellington. It turns out a lot of readers in Dallas wanted to know how their fellow Americans out in the country were doing and feeling. By Christmas of 1934, a Dallas newspaper offered Father a job. He accepted it.

Mother was happy to leave. She liked her home and her friends in Wellington. However, she was worried about James. He had never really gotten better after his "summer cold." His legs were weak. No matter what Mabel Entringer and Mother did, they were never the same. He had a hard time walking. Mabel came to our house two or three times a week, giving James exercises. She thought James had had an attack of polio, even though the doctor never said so.

Mother wanted to get to Dallas where the doctors were

better, and maybe James had a chance to get better. Mabel came with us to Dallas.

After a while, Father bought her a train ticket back home to Excelsior Springs, Missouri. When we said goodbye, Mabel said she might stay in Excelsior Springs, and not go back to Wellington. I think of Mabel a lot. I miss her.

Just before we left Wellington, a terrible winter storm came. We had snow for the first time in many years. The wind and snow were terrible. Ranchers lost cattle. It was too cold for any living thing to be outside. Bill Healy, worried about his friend Cal Meade, went out the morning after the storm. He found Cal dead outside his little house. There wasn't much food in the house, and no way to keep warm. No one could understand why Cal had gone outside during such a terrible storm.

"Maybe he heard something, and got confused by the cold," Father said.

Many years later, Father told me how hungry he'd seen Cal that summer night in 1933. He brought bread and canned food to the newspaper office to give Cal many times. But after Cal died, he thought Cal had given his food away to others he thought needed it more.

I never saw a man so sad as Bill Healy. He cried when he came to the house to tell us about Cal. Bill, Father, and Mother raised money for Cal's funeral. He was buried not far from the Booker T. Washington School. Father told Bill that maybe it was time to leave Wellington. Bill thought so, too. Father helped Bill get a job at his newspaper in Dallas. Bill stayed on at the newspaper for many years.

James and I loved Dallas. It was a big change from Wellington. I made new friends and went to high school. When I turned 18, in 1941, I started at Texas Woman's University. I studied nutrition—because of Mabel.

Of course, by 1940 and 1941, some terrible changes were taking place in the world. Like the hard times of the 1930s, they touched everyone. Jilly Kellerman, her mother, and sister Bettina were visiting family in Germany during the summer of 1939. War broke out, and Mrs. Kellerman got boat tickets to leave. She couldn't wait to get her girls back to Wellington. By that time, Bettina met a young German man and fell in love. She wouldn't leave. She slipped away one night and got married.

After weeks of arguing, Mrs. Kellerman couldn't do more. She and Jilly left Bettina behind. Bettina was killed in 1944 near the end of the war. I stayed in touch with Jilly. When I heard the news I took the train to Wellington to stay with the Kellermans. The family was ruined. Mr. and Mrs. Kellerman hardly spoke over dinner, they were so sad. Jilly told me, "I should have argued harder." I wasn't sure about that. Jilly could put up a good argument. If she couldn't get Bettina to come home, no one could.

To escape the Kellerman's terrible sadness, I walked around Wellington. I sat down in the courthouse square, and I heard someone call out, "Caitlin!" It took me a few minutes to recognize Billy Rangle. His family had stayed in Wellington. They still had their ranch beside the Salt Fork of the Red River, north of town.

Billy had grown up. He looked good. He had gone off to war in 1942, and went to Italy to fight the Germans. He was shot three times, and lost his left foot. Sitting in the courthouse square, I hadn't noticed. He was very handsome, and stood tall. One thing led to another, and "Reader, I married him."

We lived in Oklahoma City for a few years after the war ended in 1945. It won't surprise you that Billy wanted to return to the family ranch in Wellington. I was happy to go with him, and we live here now. Father and Mother visit sometimes, and so does James. He had to miss the war because of his weak legs. Instead, he became an engineer. He designs and builds bridges and highways. He is married and has a daughter.

Billy and I are happy together. We built a new house, with electricity, and now we live here with our two young children. Would you believe that we still have Billy's pa's beautiful horse, Jacko? He's very old. We don't ride him. He just eats green grass by the side of the river. We have trees, and there's shade. Life is good.

Sitting outside on a summer night, it is so quiet. You can hear the wind in the trees, and insects singing. If the wind is right, you can hear the train all the way over in Wellington. Who would ever know that on June 10, 1933, Bonnie Parker and Clyde Barrow, the two most dangerous people of our time, visited our town? I think of my all my friends then, Jilly, Katrina, Bettina, Mabel, Cal Meade, Bill Healy, Judge and Mrs. Welton, and Mr. Elms. Some stayed, some left. I have to think we're all just visitors here.

AUTHOR'S NOTE

Many details of this story are true. Bonnie Parker, Clyde Barrow, and W.D. Jones, their new 17-year-old gang member, visited Wellington, Texas on Saturday, June 10, 1933. Clyde Barrow did miss a bridge detour over the Salt Fork of the Red River seven miles north of town. The car, an elegant, fast, but stolen Ford V8, plunged into the river. Those who are familiar with the river, or really *any* river in that part of Texas, will know that there is not much water flowing most times of the year. Rather, the water is more like a meandering stream over a wide, damp bed of sand and mud. As a result, unless a river in West Texas is in full flood, one is not likely to drown. In fact, the Ford V8 still had its rear wheels up on the riverbank. According to local accounts, it was easily pulled out and repaired.

Bonnie Parker was burned badly, probably by battery acid. Without proper medical treatment, even by the standards of her time, she became unable to walk. Her leg had "drawn up," which is something modern physical therapy would have worked to counteract. She was a heavy smoker.

It was never known why Clyde Barrow missed the bridge detour. The accident is considered odd by many. Clyde Barrow was known to drive fast in stolen V8s, which is how he evaded capture so many times. He was also known as a skilled driver. I have suggested a purely fictional cause for the accident, that of a child's blue play ball rolling around at the whims of the Texas Panhandle winds. Once again, for anyone who knows West Texas, shifting, strong winds are a central feature of day to day life. It is not unusual to see objects such as balls, plastic bags, and tumbleweeds rolling across the highways, and in parks and towns. The blue ball of this story was actually seen "escaping" a sporting goods store and crossing a highway by way of a nearby cemetery, with a strong wind behind it.

Truth be told, Clyde Barrow was difficult to write about. He was a very scary guy. He was armed with guns stolen from U.S. Army facilities, and he was more than ready to shoot. In fact, he did open fire on the Wellington, Texas family who had helped him get Bonnie out of the wrecked Ford V8. One only has to read the first-hand account of Jack Pritchard, Sr., to sense how quickly the situation devolved into confusion and then violence. The Pritchards were incredibly lucky. The sole casualty was a daughter-in-law of the family who was shot in the hand through the door while holding a baby. Many reports suggested Clyde Barrow could be charming over the course of his criminal career. But I focused finally on his tired, angry, hard eyes in his later mug shots. He does not look like a man anyone in their right mind would cross. I wrote him up as such. Again, this is fiction.

This story is only nominally about Bonnie Parker and Clyde Barrow. The story is really about the people living in Wellington, Texas in the 1930s. I visited Wellington on a whim some years ago, and by accident found one of the best local museums in the region. Collingsworth County Museum is one of the few regularly open museums for a town of Wellington's size. This is largely due to efforts of the curator, Mrs. Doris Stallins. The museum has many rare documents and first-hand accounts that made this story possible. I am deeply grateful to Mrs. Stallins for putting up with my many questions, and helping put together documents for me to read. As Lubbock was three hours away, my time spent at the museum was precious.

The people of Wellington endured a great deal during the Great Depression of the 1930s. Up until that time, the county had many newcomers who had been attracted by cheap land for farming and ranching. In 1900, around 1,233 people lived in the county. By 1930, the number had exploded to 14,461. But by 1940, the end of the Great Depression, the number had gone down to 10,331. In 2017, there were 2,987 people in Collingsworth County. This reflects a downward trend experienced by many rural towns and county seats in West Texas.

As the Depression deepened, people in the Panhandle were further buffeted by dust storms and a lack of rain. One theme emerging in many first-hand accounts is farmers and ranchers being unable to keep up with loan payments to banks. They simply couldn't make a go of it. At some point, many townspeople in Wellington must have wondered whether they ought to stay. They had started out with great hopes and early farming successes, but then were faced with heartbreaking disappointment and hardship. I wanted to raise the issue of who really were "the visitors" in this story. Were they Bonnie and Clyde, or were they the townspeople themselves? I leave open this question to the reader.

Wellington now has a stable population, and has a viable downtown. It has fared better than many county seats, which are simply emptying out, even today. Wellington is a great place to visit, and to live.

Caitlin Hodges' line about sunsets comes from Louisa Anne Meredith, *My Home in Tasmania*, published in 1853. Retrieved March 26, 2019 from: https://www.atlasobscura.com/articles/overthetop-sunset-descriptions-of-history

The two books Jilly and Caitlin argue about, *Emil and the Detectives*, and *The Midnight Folk*, are in fact best-selling children's books of the early 1930s. They are both well worth a read.

There was a school for African American children in Wellington, founded and built by African Americans. It was the Booker T. Washington School. It is now a ruin, but is easily visible today: http://www.preservationtexas.org/endangered/booker-t-washington-school/ Reading about the lives of African Americans in the 1920s and 1930s in Oklahoma and Texas is deeply enriching but also deeply unsettling. The region was in Jim Crow territory. African Americans had to grow and maintain their own network of businesses and basic services, as they were not allowed entry to grocery stores, cafes, hospitals, schools, or any other place where ordinary Americans today take for granted easy entry. The character of Mabel Entringer is very loosely based on a real-life figure, that of Bobbie Nell Pipkins who was indeed a nutritionist at the Booker T. Washington School, although two decades later.

I have worked with the following paper and ink sources:

- Brown, C.C. (1934). *History of Collingsworth County.* M.A. Thesis. School not named.
- Collingsworth County History Book Committee

(1985). *Colllingsworth County*. Dallas, TX: Taylor
Publishing Co.
- Collingsworth County Museum (2009).
  Collingsworth County, Texas History, Volume 2.
- Graham, L. (1999). *One hundred and ten years of SE
  Panhandle weather*.
- Stallins, W.D. (1985). *Daniel Mackay Tench: Gentleman
  in a cane-bottomed chair*. Cullman, AL: The Gregart Co.

I also benefitted greatly from the memoirs of Beth Mostenbocker, found in the Collingsworth County Museum. She was a child in Wellington in the 1930s. It is from her memories that I envisioned a busy town square, packed with families, horses, wagons, cars, and trucks on "grocery buying day."

There are one or two digital sources I drew from. One is freely found on YouTube, "Timewatch: The Real Bonnie and Clyde." Timewatch is a British TV series. The link is: https://www.youtube.com/watch?v=cRYp6Xos79k It is interesting to see interviews with extended Barrow and Parker family members, to see how two family lores have developed over the years. Another is also freely available on the website of the Federal Bureau of Investigation: https://www.fbi.gov/history/famous-cases/bonnie-and-clyde

There are many individuals I wish to thank. First and foremost is Doris Stallins, curator of the Collingsworth County Museum, and her husband, Mr. Stallins. Thanks to the Honorable Judge James, the County Judge of Collingsworth County, for answering my many questions. Thanks to my father, John Gorsuch, who answered my many questions about 1930s products which had blue packaging. I confirmed many of them by a visit to the Panhandle Plains Museum in Canyon, Texas.

Thanks also to my father for explaining how the old upright gas pumps worked, and also why the new V8 engines in cars were so prized by what he called "bootleggers."

Finally, thanks to my brother, Neil Gorsuch, who added to my understanding of how to write up Clyde Barrow. His intuition that a criminal like Barrow would either be a "tough guy" (offensive) or a "psychopath" (charming) was helpful to think through what I needed to write.

BOOKS IN THIS SERIES

American Chapters books by Greta Gorsuch

- *The Bee Creek Blues & Meridian*
- *Lights at Chickasaw Point & The Two Garcons*
- *Living at Trace*
- *Summer in Cimarron & Lunch at the Dixie Diner*
- *The Storm*
- *Cecilia's House & The Foraging Class*

Ebooks and paperbacks are available from your favorite online retailer. Paperbacks may also be ordered by any bookstore, using the ISBN 978-1938757785. For more information, including store links, please see our website at

http://wayzgoosepress.com/greta-gorsuch

Made in the USA
Monee, IL
30 September 2020

43604292R00069